REBUILDING
THE
REAL YOU

REBUILDING THE REAL YOU

JACK HAYFORD

Charisma
HOUSE
A STRANG COMPANY

Most SMALL CAPS STRANG COMMUNICATIONS/CHARISMA HOUSE/CHRISTIAN LIFE/
EXCEL BOOKS/FRONTLINE/REALMS/SILOAM products are available at
special quantity discounts for bulk purchase for sales promotions,
premiums, fund-raising, and educational needs. For details, write Strang
Book Group, 600 Rinehart Road, Lake Mary, Florida 32746, or telephone
(407) 333-0600.

REBUILDING THE REAL YOU by Jack Hayford
Published by Charisma House
A Strang Company
600 Rinehart Road
Lake Mary, Florida 32746
www.strangdirect.com

Design Director: Bill Johnson
Cover design by studiogearbox.com

Library of Congress Cataloging-in-Publication Data
Hayford, Jack W.
  Rebuilding the real you / Jack Hayford. -- Rev. ed.
    p. cm.
  Includes bibliographical references.
  ISBN 978-1-59979-471-6
  1. Men--Religious life. 2. Bible. O.T. Nehemiah--Devotional
literature. 3. Christian life. 4. Hayford, Jack W. I. Title.
  BV4528.2.H38 2009
  248.4--dc22

                        2008041840

First published by Gospel Light, copyright © 1986. Revised edition
published by Jack Hayford Ministries, copyright © 2003, ISBN
0-91687-36-5.

09 10 11 12 13 — 987654321
Printed in the United States of America

CONTENTS

PREFACE

THE BOOK OF NEHEMIAH has become a kind of "handbook on personal restoration" for millions of people who have studied it with me.

Buried as it is at the end of the Old Testament historical books, it seems to be an unlikely prospect for contemporary relevance. If I had planned to teach a series on the ministry of the Holy Spirit to the individual believer, it would never have occurred to me to turn to Nehemiah.

I never would have expected much from this short, crusty arrangement of ancient historical events, except for a peculiar confluence of two events that took place many years ago while I was serving as senior pastor of The Church On The Way in Van Nuys, California.

After church one day, Dan, one of our congregation's elders, stopped me. "Jack, I was thinking about the number of people who are reborn but who have such a great difficulty getting their lives together. I felt the Lord impress me that I was to encourage you to bring a series of messages on that subject—something about the repairing of the human personality."

I stared back rather blankly, then replied, "Well sure, I'll keep open to it—try to keep sensitive, that is."

"That's good enough for me, Pastor," Dan replied. "I'll pray for the Lord to give you something."

Three weeks later, my wife, Anna, and I were invited to minister in Illinois. While there at this midwinter conference, we were provided with a picture-postcard setting for our accommodations— on a small hilltop in the country, surrounded by snow-bedecked trees. It was a scene from a Currier and Ives print, delightfully suited for a few days away from our daily responsibilities. I decided to do some aggressive Bible reading.

Now, by "aggressive" I mean the rapid coverage of long passages of Scripture. It's so easy in the daily study of briefer passages to miss the grand panorama of whole segments of the Word. So it was there, comfortably ensconced before the fire in a cozy setting, that I spent hours at a time reading with reasonable speed through the twelve history books of the Old Testament.

I swept through exciting territory—the dynamics, the drama, and the disasters of Israel's rise and fall as a kingdom. Then I came to Nehemiah.

I seriously pondered skipping it.

Of course, I had studied the book during my formal training and had read it a few times in through-the-Bible pursuits. It was, to my understanding, simply the historical record of the efforts of one man to assist the Jews who had returned from Babylonian captivity in the rebuilding of the walls of the city of Jerusalem. I knew the content: I was aware that there were several chapters with nothing more than boring lists and historical reviews. I was about to go on to the next book when I was prompted to stop and reconsider.

As I did, I prayed, "Lord, I don't ever want to take any part of Your Word carelessly. I'm going to read this brief book rather than skip past it, but I'm asking You a favor: as I read, would You show me something fresh in it? Thank You, Lord. In Jesus's name, amen."

I meant the prayer, but my faith was not particularly active in terms of my feeling expectant as I began to read. So as I started, I wasn't looking for something special, new, clever, or insightful. What happened was simply the result of our loving Father's gift to me.

I had read about three chapters when suddenly a sense of holy surprise came over me. I paused, musing, "This wall-rebuilding process is very close to being a picture of the way God restores people." Immediately Dan's words flew back to mind, and I laughed to myself, "I'll bet he's been praying." I finished Nehemiah and Esther, the remaining books of Old Testament history, scratching notes in the margins as I read and becoming very deeply impressed with the possibilities of the subject.

I came home and began an extended sermon series in our midweek services at the church. The tapes of that series became a staple in our church's pastoral counseling ministry, and they were distributed widely. Our staff provided the tapes to assist people to recover from distress resulting from past experiences. Through the ministry of World MAP, a mission assistance agency, I was allowed to present the teaching series not only at one of their summer conferences but also through their global tape ministry to leaders on every continent. Mail began to increase, attesting to the validity of these insights from Nehemiah. The Word of God was working in people's lives.

Then, through the widespread ministry of the Christian Broadcasting Network in the early 1980s, I was invited to do the series via a weekly telecast, and the teaching reached out to countless more people. In my visits around the country, I started hearing from people everywhere I went about God's grace at work in them through that series on Nehemiah—so unlikely a source, yet so alive because it is His eternal Word. Later, the Trinity Broadcasting Network carried an even more expanded video edition to millions.

I cannot begin to enumerate the number of dear people who have expressed the life-transforming, Christ-glorifying dimensions of renewal and personal restoration they have experienced through the study to which I now invite you. I feel like a third person, looking in on a teaching session, watching the Holy Spirit take truth and apply it from His eternal Word into your situations. It's a privilege to be the delivery boy of this message. How fulfilling is the prospect; this study can enable the Holy Spirit's highest and greatest ministry to be realized in you.

Introduction

REBUILDING THE REAL YOU

HIS IS NOT A self-help book. Neither is it a structured Bible study of the Book of Nehemiah.

But this is a book about help, or better yet, about a Helper. The best part is that the help He has is for *you*, and the Book of Nehemiah can provide you with a picture of how He wants to help you.

Therefore, far from being a self-help book, this is a book about how to partner with the Holy Spirit on your personal renewal project, which is something that He has wanted to help you with since before you were born again.

Self-help books usually mislead because they promise too much and provide too little. In all self-improvement books, the fundamental grounds for hope are humankind—you, me, us, we. As "self-helpers," we may not be all that bad, but we're not really good enough. When you start with human beings, all you're going to get is human help. Even though the presumption survives that people have what it takes, the evidence is in; the fact is, it isn't enough.

This book's foundational proposition is that there is a genuine possibility of personal restoration and fulfillment for everyone, regardless of what your past may hold, but that personal restoration can only occur at the invitation of the Holy Spirit and under His ongoing tutelage.

We have all experienced something of brokenness: hearts, homes, health, finance, dreams, relationships—all as breakable as bones, though harder to set. We may not all be basket cases, but it's certain we all need the Doctor.

The Doctor is God, who is larger than any brokenness and is the fountainhead of life itself. He is the Father of love, and He has the right to speak with authority to His children. He has given us His Word, and He enlivens it to our human hearts.

He sent the Messiah, Jesus, and He has proven the Messiah's miraculous capacity for meeting our needs by raising Him from the dead and sending His Holy Spirit to dwell in our hearts. In the context of the reality of the Messiah's resurrection, there is nothing impossible for your life or mine.

The Holy Spirit has come to glorify Jesus, the Son of God. Jesus is glorified most of all through our human personalities. The Father created us in splendor, in His own image, but that splendor has been badly marred. Jesus came to redeem the Father's original intention in us and through us.

I believe that you believe this too, because I believe everyone has faith: "As God has dealt to each one a measure of faith" (Rom. 12:3). I am not saying that everyone's faith is perfect, accurate, or functional. But it is there.

In fact, it takes studied effort and a deep commitment to *not* believe, for faith can rarely be crowded out of a human soul.

Disaster may burn it, tragedy may smash it, injury may bruise it, or arrogance may denounce it. But faith, like seed buried under concrete, is difficult to keep down permanently.

Your faith is probably ready. Your faith may be active, alive, and vibrant enough to respond to the truth of God's eternal Word and His risen Son.

Let me encourage you to welcome a new dimension of "help" into your life—the help I referred to at the beginning and that comes in the person of a Helper.

His first name is "Holy," and He is the Spirit of God, called the Holy Spirit. He is as truly and completely God as either the Father or the Son. He is deeply personal, all-powerful, and ever present. He wants to make Himself known in the details of your life.

He is one of the Three-in-One, but don't worry if you don't understand such theological elements. He doesn't mind our human limitations, because the Holy Spirit—indeed, God in any aspect of His person—is fully secure enough to be comfortable with our finite understanding. He isn't running a heavenly quiz to see how much we know, for in the last analysis, our salvation and our destiny will not be resolved by how much we know but by whom we know.

His mission—and He's decided to accept it!—is to maximize your potential by helping you to truly "get it all together." I think your perspective on both yourself and the Holy Spirit will be broadened and deepened as you pursue these pages. As we examine how the seldom-read Book of Nehemiah presents a beautifully encoded picture of the Holy Spirit's person, style, and ministry, we will be able to participate in the rebuilding of our own souls.

The Helper is ready to bring you to fulfillment and to your highest destiny.

Historical Nehemiah—Picture of the Holy Spirit

The Book of Nehemiah was written about four and a half centuries before the birth and life, death, and resurrection of Jesus Christ, and yet the Holy Spirit, who is timeless, was making sure that we would have a vibrant portrayal of His work in human lives.

The Bible says:

> All Scripture is given by inspiration of God, and is profitable for doctrine, for reproof, for correction, for instruction in righteousness, that the man of God may be complete, thoroughly equipped for every good work.
>
> —2 Timothy 3:16–17

This clearly argues against the opinion of some teachers that historical books of the Bible cannot be sources of establishing truth, in other words, doctrine. The New Testament word *doctrine* (*didaskalia*) simply means "teaching." There are at least three types of teachings most Old Testament historical books contain:

1. Facts concerning the past
2. Moral and spiritual lessons
3. Pictures of New Testament truth

Nehemiah contains all three, and my expositional approach to this book includes an unfolding of a very clear picture of the nature and work of the Holy Spirit assisting the believer in rebuilding the broken places of human life. This is consistent with the expository style of several New Testament writers and is verified by the clear statements of the Word concerning the content of the Old Testament as it bears on our lives today:

> For whatever things were written before were written for our learning, that we through the patience and comfort of the Scriptures might have hope.
>
> —ROMANS 15:4

> Now all these things happened to them as examples, and they were written for our admonition, on whom the ends of the ages have come.
>
> —1 CORINTHIANS 10:11

I have not tried to cover of the Book of Nehemiah exhaustively, since much of its content is historical information only. Nehemiah contains 13 chapters and 406 verses. Of the verses, 189 list names, 38 recite earlier history, and 179 describe Nehemiah's actions. In this book, I have elaborated on less than half of the actual content of the Book of Nehemiah, concerned as I am largely with Nehemiah himself, his work, his leadership, and his influence.

The Book of Nehemiah begins in the year 446 B.C., ninety years since more than fifty thousand Jews had been released by the edict of Cyrus, ruler of the Medo-Persians. Through the leadership of a remarkable man named Zerubbabel, they had returned to Jerusalem. To say "they" returned refers to the Jews as a people, for, in fact, very few of the contingent who returned had ever been there before.

The returning exiles were actually the children and grandchildren of people who had been taken captive during the conquest and ultimate destruction of Jerusalem by the renowned Nebuchadnezzar, dreaded monarch of ancient Babylon. Consistent with the methods of conquerors in that era, he had not only leveled and burned their capital city, but he had also sought to totally break their spirit by taking them captive. He removed them from their homeland to a distant culture, hoping thereby to dissolve their identity as a people and smash their will as individuals.

Prior to this destruction and actual exiling of these Jews, Nebuchadnezzar had earlier gained dominion over Judea and its capital city, Jerusalem. He had installed puppet kings to govern the area, to keep it both accountable to and taxable by him. But due to recurrent resistance and political rebellion against his government, the decision was finally made to sack the city and exile any remaining prisoners to Babylon.

During that period of the puppet kings Jehoiakim and Zedekiah, the prophet Jeremiah warned of judgment to come because of the Jews' willful disregard to live as God commanded. Jeremiah had even predicted the length of their captivity: seventy years. He further prophesied that after this period of time, the exiled people would be released to return to Jerusalem to restore their temple and their worship of God. (See Jeremiah 25:11; 29:10.)

GREAT PROPHECIES FULFILLED

International events wove together in an amazing combination, and the great prophecies by Isaiah, Ezekiel, Zephaniah, and Haggai were fulfilled. The balance of world power had swung from Babylon to Persia, and the fate of the exiled Jews went into the hands of those who had conquered their conquerors. In this swirl of prophetic and historic activities God was at work restoring His people, while nations and their kings unwittingly bowed to the performance of His will.

The result was the release of all Jews who wished to return to Jerusalem. Cyrus issued the edict according to Isaiah's prophecy, a forecast that was all the more phenomenal in view of the fact that the prophet had named the ruler who would release the exiles a century before the man was even born! (See Isaiah 44:28; Ezra 1:1–4.) The prophet Ezekiel, who had lived with the people through their captive experience in the regions of Babylon, also foretold their return and the reconstruction of their temple.

Given the complexity of the situation, it would seem all the more unlikely that their release should be realized. But deliverance came right on schedule. In the year 536 B.C.—exactly seventy years after the first contingent of exiles had come to Babylon—Cyrus ordered their release.

Nehemiah's words "the Jews who had escaped," refer to those who, by the emperor's decree, were allowed to return and to begin rebuilding their city and their nation. As a people, they would never be the same. The impact of the Babylonian captivity on the Jews had one positive result: polytheism, the worship of many gods, was forever expelled from their minds. Henceforth, only the Lord

Jehovah would be their God, and Moses's words would live in their minds, as they do in ours to the present: "Hear, O Israel: The LORD our God, the LORD is one!" (Deut. 6:4; Mark 12:29).

Accordingly, upon return, their first major undertaking was to rebuild the temple in Jerusalem. They were a people for whom the pure worship of the one true God was a priority. Ezra, that small book just preceding Nehemiah, records this rebuilding (Ezra 3–6). Ezra reported not only the return and rebuilding of the temple, but he also described the difficulties encountered in that project—obstacles that were overcome through the spiritual inspirations of the prophets Zechariah and Haggai.

It took twenty years from the inception of the project, but finally the temple was completed and dedicated in the year 516 B.C. (See Ezra 6:15.) The promise of the Lord had returned to a formerly desolated people, and their restored relationship with the living God was manifested in the rebuilt temple to which they would gather for joyous worship.

THE JEWS' EMBARRASSMENT

After that, however, two more generations elapsed. Ninety years later since they returned and seventy years since their completion of the temple, the Jew Nehemiah, who was an important official in the Persian Empire, discovers that his ancestral city was still without walls. His people had been able to reestablish their worship, but they lacked the evidence of a reestablished rulership—a respectable capital city rising above the ashes of its past destruction. With nearly a century behind them, there seemed to be little reason for this embarrassing situation. How justly might surrounding nations and peoples mock them: "Some God, Jehovah! What power do you attribute to a God whose worshipers live like squatters?"

News of this situation occasioned deep grief and growing concern in Nehemiah. The city had no walls; it was a blight upon the name of its people and a reproach upon the name of their God. Nehemiah, weeping, mourning, and fasting, began to pray.

The character of this man, who is introduced to us in the first chapter of the Book of Nehemiah as a cupbearer or consultant to the Persian emperor Artaxerxes, is profoundly evidenced by his actions. His concern for his people—that they be established, strengthened, and respected as a stable nation—transcends his concerns for his own security, prestige, or convenience. We will find him interceding (Neh. 1), risking his life and obligating himself in their interest (Neh. 2), securing their safety (Neh. 4), unselfishly giving of his own resources (Neh. 5), committing himself to the completion of a task that will remove their shame (Neh. 6), and more.

In meeting Nehemiah and in looking at what he did for the Jews, a picture of the Holy Spirit emerges.

Let's turn our attention directly to Him first, and then begin to explore how the Book of Nehemiah can show us how to partner with the Holy Spirit through the often-challenging task of rebuilding the "walls" of our lives.

Part One

WHAT NEEDS REBUILDING?

The words of Nehemiah the son of Hachaliah. It came to pass in the month of Chislev, in the twentieth year, as I was in Shushan the citadel, that Hanani one of my brethren came with men from Judah; and I asked them concerning the Jews who had escaped, who had survived the captivity, and concerning Jerusalem. And they said to me, "The survivors who are left from the captivity in the province are there in great distress and reproach. The wall of Jerusalem is also broken down, and its gates are burned with fire."

So it was, when I heard these words, that I sat down and wept, and mourned for many days; I was fasting and praying before the God of heaven.

And I said: "I pray, LORD God of heaven, O great and awesome God, You who keep Your covenant and mercy with those who love You and observe Your commandments, please let Your ear be attentive and Your eyes open, that You may hear the prayer of Your servant which I pray before You now, day and night, for the children of Israel Your servants, and confess the sins of the children of Israel which we have sinned against You. Both my father's house and I have sinned. We have acted very corruptly against

You, and have not kept the commandments, the statutes, nor the ordinances which You commanded Your servant Moses. Remember, I pray, the word that You commanded Your servant Moses, saying, 'If you are unfaithful, I will scatter you among the nations; but if you return to Me, and keep My commandments and do them, though some of you were cast out to the farthest part of the heavens, yet I will gather them from there, and bring them to the place which I have chosen as a dwelling for My name.' Now these are Your servants and Your people, whom You have redeemed by Your great power, and by Your strong hand. O Lord, I pray, please let Your ear be attentive to the prayer of Your servant, and to the prayer of Your servants who desire to fear Your name; and let Your servant prosper this day, I pray, and grant him mercy in the sight of this man."

For I was the king's cupbearer.

And it came to pass in the month of Nisan, in the twentieth year of King Artaxerxes, when wine was before him, that I took the wine and gave it to the king. Now I had never been sad in his presence before. Therefore the king said to me, "Why is your face sad, since you are not sick? This is nothing but sorrow of heart."

So I became dreadfully afraid, and said to the king, "May the king live forever! Why should my face not be sad, when the city, the place of my fathers' tombs, lies waste, and its gates are burned with fire?"

Then the king said to me, "What do you request?"

So I prayed to the God of heaven. And I said to the king, "If it pleases the king, and if your servant has found favor in your sight, I ask that you send me to Judah, to the city of my fathers' tombs, that I may rebuild it."

Then the king said to me (the queen also sitting beside him), "How long will your journey be? And when will you return?" So it pleased the king to send me; and I set him a time.

—NEHEMIAH 1:1–11; 2:1–6

Chapter 1

MEETING A FOREVER FRIEND

The Holy Spirit, the third person of the Trinity—Father, Son, and Holy Spirit—is somewhat of a mystery to most people. Referred to for centuries as the Holy Ghost, a dimension of unreality, if not spookiness, has surrounded His person for a long time.

The Holy Spirit is personal. He is God, a "He," not an "it." He is not some abstract force or distant cosmic influence. The Holy Spirit is one expression of the God who created us, loves us, redeemed us, and longs to bring us to full maturity in life, to the realization of His created purpose in each of us.

Jesus shed a great deal of light on the personality of the Holy Spirit when He taught us that: (1) He is like Jesus Himself in character, temperament, and works (John 14:17), (2) His mission is to help us personally understand more and more about Jesus (John 16:14), and (3) He has come to abide—to stay with us, somewhat of a heaven-sent forever friend (John 14:16). The most cursory reading of John's Gospel, chapters 14 to 16, establishes this. The Holy Spirit is sent by the Father, in the name of the Son, to be with each one of us and to help us. There's nothing spooky about that.

The Holy Spirit Enters at New Birth

When a person comes to God the Father and willingly receives the gift of life through Jesus the Son, the first thing that happens is that the Holy Spirit enters that person's life. Jesus described Him as a "Comforter"—One who will remain beside you to help, to counsel, to teach, and to strengthen you. His entering is only a beginning, though, and the sensible believer in the Lord Jesus will keep open to the Holy Spirit's increasing desire to expand the evidence of God's purposes in his or her life.

The fullness of the Holy Spirit, the fruit of the Holy Spirit, the gifts of the Holy Spirit, and, most of all, the abundant, flowing love of the Holy Spirit are all expressions of God's intent in giving us His Spirit. In other words, to simply realize that the Holy Spirit entered when I received Christ is to grasp a precious truth. But I need to see more—to want more. The practical development of God's work in my life requires that I give a growing place to the Holy Spirit's working within me. The Comforter has come, and His mission is to help us move forward as growing sons and daughters of the Most High God.

In the Word of God, we can see how to test the validity of the Spirit's presence and work in a believer's life: He makes people more thankful, more loving, more generous, more considerate, more understanding—in short, more like Jesus. Since our study will have a great deal to say about the Holy Spirit's work in our lives, let us understand from the beginning that the whole objective is not to displace Jesus with an emphasis on the Holy Spirit, but to replace our weakness and personal inadequacy with the Holy Spirit's enabling presence. In this way, Jesus Christ will be seen more perfectly in each of us.

Even among people who have experienced the entry of the Holy Spirit into their lives—that is, people who have received God's love and forgiveness through Christ's death and resurrection—there seems to be wide variations in response to the Holy Spirit. Some hesitate in their readiness or their ability to allow the Holy Spirit an ever-increasing breadth of space to work in their lives. Such hesitation or apparent inability often seems related to a person's depth of difficulty with life prior to his or her conversion.

We are notorious for not asking for God's help until our backs are against the wall. Somehow, we have been persuaded either that we can manage by ourselves or that to "bother" God for anything other than a crisis condition would somehow impinge upon His patience. This habit of waiting until our circumstances are drastic usually means that by the time we finally open our lives to Christ, considerable damage has been done. The net result is that whatever our past, however gifted our capacity at survival, virtually all of us badly need the Holy Spirit's restoring work in our lives. That work begins when we welcome Him to take charge of the rebuilding process. That process advances as He is permitted full rein—and full reign.

If you have never opened up to the beginning of God's Spirit working deeply and powerfully in you, the path to that entrance is through one clearly marked door: Jesus Christ, God's Son. He said, "I am the door.... I am the way.... No one comes to the Father except through Me....Nor is there salvation in any other, for there is no other name under heaven given among men by which we must be saved" (John 10:9; 14:6; Acts 4:12). To open your life to Jesus Christ is to welcome the Holy Spirit into your life at the same time, for "no one can say that Jesus is Lord except by the Holy Spirit" (1 Cor. 12:3). Simple heartfelt prayer can establish a turning from your own way unto His. (See Appendix C if you want to be sure that you have been reborn and filled with the Holy Spirit.) From this beginning, your life is waiting to unfold in the will of God and by the Spirit of God.

The Holy Spirit Directs Growth

Having begun life in Christ Jesus, we shortly confront a crucial question: Having begun this life by the power of the Holy Spirit, how shall we grow in this new life? The answer is rather obvious: by the power of the same Spirit! But most of us are slow to understand this fact.

Paul asked the Galatians, "After starting your Christian lives in the Spirit, why are you now trying to become perfect by your own human effort?" (Gal. 3:3, NLT). We all need the same reminder: New birth isn't the end of God's program for us. His Spirit has started something by His power that He wants to advance with our partnership.

Now, everything I have said up to now is probably easy enough for you to acknowledge. Any honest believer will be quick to say, "I need to grow," or "I want to grow." But the pathway to growth is usually cluttered with obstacles, and the obstacles are usually hang-overs from our past—past lifestyle, past habits, past attitudes, past sinning. We will not "grow out of" such things naturally. It's the partnership with the Holy Spirit that is all-important to our spiritual and emotional growth.

In other words, the results of our past all too often remain part of our present reality. The fact that you sinned in the past can be seen in its remaining fruit. Of course, you can be absolutely certain that God has forgiven it all: this is a bright truth of your new God-given inheritance! But of equal certainty is the continuing presence of many personal problems bequeathed to you from your past. Your salvation solves the problem of your relationship with God, but it doesn't always dissolve the problems in your life. It opens the doorway to solutions, but it is only by walking through that door and patiently pursuing that way that those problems will finally be resolved.

NEHEMIAH: THE CONSOLATION OF GOD

This fact stands out so clearly in the Book of Nehemiah. Here is the story of a people who had been given a new lease on life but who were repeatedly embarrassed by their inability to demonstrate complete evidence of renewal. Their rebirth was in their return to their ancestral land, but their recovery as a people was incomplete, a fact underscored by their inability to restore their capital city. It appeared that it would never happen. Having heard of their distress, a kinsman and leader named Nehemiah came from a distant land to begin—and to complete—the rebuilding process by which the walls of Jerusalem would be restored from the rubble of past destruction.

Nehemiah was sent by the king, just as the Holy Spirit has been sent to us by our King, the Lord Jesus.

Nehemiah's work was to lead. He didn't do the whole job on his own, but rather he taught the people how to move forward together in the rebuilding project. In much the same way, the Holy Spirit comes to help us rebuild our personal lives from the rubble of their past destruction.

Nehemiah brought authority to a downtrodden people, authority that engendered confidence and rose effectively against the adversaries of the rebuilding project. Nehemiah is a picture of the Holy Spirit at work.

I discovered this definition in my Hebrew lexicon: "Nehemiah—the consolation of God—derived from *nacham*, to breathe strongly, to pity, to console; and from *Yah*, the sacred name of the Lord." In short, Nehemiah means "the consoling breath or spirit of God." Further background study revealed his name was built from a verb root that conveys the idea of "pity that becomes active in the interest of another." In other words, not only is Nehemiah is a good picture of the Holy Spirit, but also his name is virtually synonymous with His! Nehemiah is like the Comforter.

Could it be that centuries before the coming of Jesus—long before He gave His people the gift of the Holy Spirit—God had implanted in His own Word a coded message about the Holy Spirit's ministry of recovery? Could it be that forecast in this piece of Israel's history, just as other spiritual truths were prefigured Old Testament events, a message of salvation's fuller provisions was foreshadowed? Could it be that the historical person Nehemiah, without realizing it himself, was the key figure in a timeless moving picture about the way God's Spirit assists us in the recovery of all those ruined parts of our lives that sin has disintegrated?

For all of the rich truths it contains—historic information, practical truths concerning leadership, worthwhile principles for Christian living—Nehemiah is also a handbook on the pathway to personal restoration. The Book of Nehemiah is an ideal guidebook. Here's how the Holy Spirit comes to assist us in rebuilding our brokenness, strengthening our weaknesses, and leading us past our ignorance and into victory.

We are people who need more than rebirth—we need rebuilding as well. Our Savior has sent His Holy Spirit to partner with us in the rebuilding of every part of our lives.

Chapter 2

ESTABLISHED, STRENGTHENED, SETTLED

<hr>

W HAT HAPPENED WHEN MAN 'fell'?" the Sunday school teacher asked the little boy.

"I don't know," he answered with a puzzled expression. "Did he bounce?"

Most people have a better idea than that of what is meant by the "fall of man," yet it is important to our study that we have an agreed viewpoint on this foundational event in human history.

The Fall summarizes in two words the fact that God designed men and women with a higher estate and an innately superior destiny than they now generally experience or realize, and that the entry of sin into the world changed everything drastically. People, created perfectly "in the image of God" (Gen. 1:27), were designed for large purposes and deep fulfillment. If people were to reflect God's nature, which includes the feature of free will, the capacity of human beings for self-will (even for disobedience) was not an inherent flaw but rather a necessary part of human makeup.

The opening chapters of Genesis tell us three essential truths:

1. Man was created in God's image and with unimaginably high destiny and purpose.

2. Man was given responsible dominion over the earth—a rule to be expressed in everything from family relationships to the subjugation of Earth and its resources through creative development.

3. Man's authority and ability to successfully exercise that rule would find its fountainhead in continued obedience to and worshipful relationship with his Creator.

So we see that relationship and rulership are fundamental to our created purpose, and both have been broken by the Fall. Without recovery, our Creator's design for us cannot be fulfilled. Until the impact of the Fall is dealt with, we will be unable to truly live, find fulfillment, or experience His purpose in and through us.

It is important for you to grasp a sense of the dimensions of loss in the Fall, for unless you perceive something of what has been lost, you won't know what you might expect to regain through the full salvation of Jesus Christ.

The Beginning of God's Redemptive Purpose

For the most part, Christian preaching and teaching focus only on restoring people to a relationship with God: showing how the cross of Jesus Christ has bridged the chasm that sin has caused between God and man and how salvation offers man a way back to God. Of course, this message is absolutely necessary and is fundamental as a starting point of understanding. We must be born again (John 3:3).

But if we just stop there at the acknowledgment of our need for a restored relationship, we may fail to perceive God's full redemptive purpose for fallen man. The restored relationship is primary in sequence, but salvation alone does not conclude God's purpose in life for us. His desire is to return us to restored rulership. This means a recovery of self-control, of personal identity, of stabilized temperament and character. It means the fulfillment of Romans 5:17, that "those who receive abundance of grace and of the gift of righteousness will reign in life through the One, Jesus Christ."

Grace in action results in a life that has been restored to its original purpose, one that has been established, strengthened, and settled:

> May the God of all grace, who called us to His eternal glory by Christ Jesus, after you have suffered a while, perfect, establish, strengthen, and settle you.
>
> —1 PETER 5:10

The essence of the rebuilding project does not focus on a restored relationship so much as it does a restored rule—the recovery of a godly people's identity as self-governing and their city's restored appearance as a capital center of righteousness. Instead of dwelling amid the rubble of the once-glorious city of Jerusalem, the people will learn to rule in their daily lives.

Distress and Reproach

The opening conversation between Nehemiah and Hanani, a relative who visited him with a report from the returned exiles in Jerusalem, reveals the crux of concern:

"How is it going with our brethren who have returned to Judah?" Nehemiah asked.

"Those who have returned are in great distress and reproach," Hanani replied.

"What is the cause of their problem?" Nehemiah probed further.

"The wall of Jerusalem is broken down and its gates are burned," revealed Hanani.

Hanani's complaint focused on the embarrassment of a people who had solid evidence of a relationship with God. God had fulfilled His Word and returned the Jews to their land. Next, He had helped them in the project of rebuilding the temple, and when it was finished, they began to conduct regular, God-honoring worship at the temple site. In other words, their relationship was restored and their worship was faithful and pure.

Notwithstanding the joy of that right relationship with God, the people recognized the incompleteness of their situation: "We have a temple, but our capital city—our center of government—is in shambles." You see, without a wall, the city was open prey to oppressors. With destroyed gates, there was no way of keeping back an adversary. There was also no focus of government, for in ancient times the city gates were the seat of local rule.

In short, they had a life with God but had no evidence of it affecting the daily details of life. They were embarrassed. After all, this was their representative city—their "face" to the world around. But even though their temple had been rebuilt, the rest of the city and the walls surrounding it were nothing but rubble. How vulnerable they were to the mockery of their critics and enemies: "Some God you worship in that temple! Look at the mess you call your capital city. Apparently your God has little concern for or no ability in the practical matters of life!"

Have you ever sensed this dilemma yourself? Are you born again, yet parts of your personality are a contradiction to the power of the God you worship? Might someone justly point a finger and challenge, "Big deal! Some new birth. Look at the mess...!"? After evaluating your life and noting how much is broken down and "burned with fire," you may feel that same sense of reproach and distress that Hanani expressed to Nehemiah. If you do, take hope. Nehemiah gives us a message about people who not only had recovered their relationship with God but who also moved on in that relationship to recover their potential to function as full citizens of the city of God, Jerusalem. They learned what it means to "reign in life," as the Bible says. Or as contemporary jargon puts it, they had "gotten it together."

The Book of Nehemiah is a handbook on recovering what's been lost by sin. Here we see a picture of the hope that our restored relationship with God (like the rebuilt temple) can be matched by a restoration of two things: (1) rulership and regained self-control (represented by the restored gates), and (2) a reconstruction of our self-understanding and purpose (represented by the rebuilt walls).

The Rubble of the Past

As a nation, Israel had walked in disobedience, and they had failed God. After many warnings and exhortations from God through the prophets, judgment came upon them.

(Lest you misunderstand, be assured that such judgment is not so much an act of God's anger as it is simply the certain result of disobedience. Father God is injured and grieved when, through rebellion or ignorance, we ignore His way in favor of pursuing our own. Yet His judgment is never vindictive. God does not even have to activate every instance of judgment upon sin, because most sin bears within itself the deadly seeds of its own penalty. When the sin is sown, the judgment comes as sure as harvest time. People have introduced judgment upon their own heads through their sin, and the destruction distilled from their failure often leaves a sad residue—even after they have been saved.)

So it was that even though Israel had returned, had built their temple, and as a people were praising their God, the surrounding rubble remained as a sad and humiliating evidence of their past sinning.

So often the same is true of us. How many are the ways in which we, the reborn, are a paradox—possessors of eternal life but dispossessed of a sense of solid personhood?

Have you ever asked yourself:

- "Why can't I shut depressive thoughts out of my mind?"
- "Why am I so shaken by fears?"

- "Why can't I defend myself against temptation?"
- "Why do I always feel so worthless?"

Shouldn't your restored relationship with God be enough to keep out unwanted thoughts and attitudes? Or is there another aspect of our salvation available and waiting to be appropriated? Can the Lord reinstate His rule in me just as He has reinstated my relationship with Him? The answer: absolutely!

The starting place is to see both the need and goal of such recovery. The time it takes for your recovery process may differ from that of other people.

PATIENCE WITH REBUILDING THE REAL YOU

Many believers have such a struggle trying to learn to walk as steadfast disciples of Christ while they remain so very crippled from their earlier life. Although in sincerity they seek to speed ahead, before long, they become frustrated and confused, especially when they see others who are progressing steadily.

As I have said, becoming a new creature in Christ is only the beginning of this new life. The promise "If any man be in Christ, he is a new creature" (2 Cor. 5:17, KJV) does not instantly guarantee completed results. It does promise a new world of possibility opening to us; we are no longer dominated or controlled by our past. But for the full dominion of Christ's rule to penetrate the whole personality, in most cases, "the real you" needs to be rebuilt.

Consider the testimony of two radically different reborn babes in Christ under my own pastoral charge.

"Terri" stepped into my office one Saturday afternoon in tears, having just been kicked out of their apartment by her husband. He was a satanist, and they had both been heavily involved in the occult before her conversion to Christ. Her past involved a great deal of rejection by her parents and personal violation by her father. Though she was highly intelligent and a product of one of America's finest universities, Terri was virtually incoherent as she stood before me in tears. Here she was, bereft of support and the mother of two lovable little children who themselves were terribly confused by what was happening with Momma and Daddy. This combination of factors shaping her present was a staggering load for a young Christian. She unquestionably was Christ's—she was reborn in Him. But the remnants of her past now converged to reduce her to an emotional basket case, a domestic wreck, and a desperate spiritual dependent. Though she was a new creature in Christ, Terri was a highly vulnerable babe who could hardly walk, completely ignorant of what to do and how to do it. "Broken walls and burned gates" would aptly describe her.

For the following five years, I watched her grow through the Word, through a fellowship with the body of the congregation, and by the assistance of wise counselors on the pastoral staff. The rebuilding process was long, but she eventually became an adequate, recovered person. Having long since been forsaken by her husband, God later provided a godly young man as His gift, completing the redemption of her domestic past. (See 1 Corinthians 7:15.) I was witness to that marriage, and I delight to tell you that in every way, Terri is restored, and her children are lovely, stable, happy kids. She has become what her name implies—an expression of "the will of God."

"Jason" was the kind of convert all pastors wish they could have in their churches. It was a joy watching Jason respond as he went from new birth to solid discipleship within several weeks of his conversion. Within months he was given some leadership roles, and within three years he moved into eldership. He was recognized within the congregation as a growing-to-strength servant of Jesus Christ.

Jason's former "walls" were considerably different from Terri's. His family background was solid and secure, and he had parents who raised him lovingly. He never knew the pain of parental rejection, and for most of his life he had experienced every cultural, financial, educational, intellectual, and emotional benefit a young man can receive. Moreover, he was raised in the context of a Christianized environment, in a church that reverenced God. Even though the Word of God and our universal need of new life in Christ were not taught there, the social influence was redemptive and moral values honored. Therefore, although Jason had never heard the message of salvation until later in his life, he did have some knowledge of the Bible and a genuine desire for spiritual reality. He was successful in business, emotionally stable, and economically and professionally secure. The simple fact is that Jason had little from which to recover.

He needed rebirth—everyone does. And he accepted discipleship, as we all should. But Jason was able to become firm in personal and spiritual stability much more rapidly than Terri, although today their relative strength in Christ is virtually equal.

The whole point of these two illustrations is to dramatize the truth that some who have been Christians for years have Terri-like problems from the past. Perhaps you do not have as desperate a situation as she did, but you certainly wish you knew how to get from where you are to where you want to be as Jesus's disciple. Sheer grit and determination are honorable while they last. But beside the fact that weariness usually takes over with time, grit and determination aren't God's way. Such so-called discipleship is nothing more than works built on grace, and, given time, the temporary walls of self-worked righteousness will crumble.

Most of us are among the vast number and variety of "Terris." "Jasons" are joyful and welcome exceptions, but very few people today have Jason's privileged background. Most of us are in considerable need of repair at the personal level (and even Jason would acknowledge points of rebuilding his own life required).

Since you will not experience the fullest extent of Christ's kingdom rule in all your life until wholeness in your personality is realized, you need to let patience perform its perfect work. Some issues can be changed overnight through simple obedience to God's Word. But other problems of personal weakness, the residue from the impact of past sinning, require time. Rebuilding alone will accomplish what rebirth makes possible but does not instantly achieve.

The rebuilding stage of Christian life involves these important aspects: First, partner with the Holy Spirit, your "Nehemiah." Second, let Him help you to identify your "broken walls and burned gates." Third, do the work necessary to rebuild the walls with the help of the Spirit as well as the people He sets you with.

If you are diligent and dedicated to the work, you will reach a point where you can say, "By God's grace, I am established, strengthened, and settled. Now I can conduct my daily affairs with success, and I can help others freely." Not only will your spirit, which used to be dead in sin, be reborn, but also your soul (your mind, emotions, and decision-making ability), which had been as broken down as the walls of Jerusalem, be restored. Wherever your walls were destroyed and you were destitute, God will establish you and make you secure by the power of His love.

As you begin, remember that those broken, burned walls of your own personality are not always the direct result of your own sin. In Jerusalem, the people had inherited that condition; it was not actually due to their own actions, for the destruction of the city was the price of another generation's failure.

Similarly, many of us have been prevented or obstructed from our "reign in life" through inherited difficulties or personality weaknesses that were "transmitted" to us from an earlier generation. At times the transmission has been through actions. Misunderstanding or mistreatment from parents or other authority figures, whether unwitting or intentional, often stamps us with lifelong scars—unless recovery occurs. Our childhood innocence has often been tainted by adult ignorance, and without redemptive action, we will suffer from permanent emotional disability. Other transmissions seem to be more "genetic" not only from a physical perspective but also from spiritual, emotional, and mental ones.

The wreckage is considerable, and it far exceeds our self-help abilities. Even sincere dedication to Christian disciplines or renunciation of bad habits cannot rebuild the toppled walls of our personalities. We hardly know what they're supposed to look like, although we recognize them as our very own once they have been rebuilt.

Come help us, Nehemiah!

Chapter 3

TEMPLE AND SPIRIT,
WALLS AND SOUL

=======================================

I'M SURE YOU HAVE dabbled with jigsaw puzzles enough to experience the irritation of discovering missing pieces. Without all of the pieces, you cannot finish the puzzle; you can't see the full picture.

Along the same lines, I've watched the frustration of people who want to "see the whole picture" of God's purpose in their lives but who don't understand how the pieces of their personality fit together. A surprising number of intelligent spiritual people have no real definition of the makeup of their personality or the constituent parts of their being.

For starters, most Christians do not know the difference between their soul and their spirit. Far more than an academic issue, the distinction between soul and spirit is just as clear as the difference between the broken walls of the city of Jerusalem and the temple built within the city. Could the temple defend the populace against invaders? Conversely, could the walls supply all that was needed for the worship of God?

Walls and temple are distinctly different, and yet each is integral to the whole, restored city. Jerusalem was incomplete without walls, even after the temple had been restored. In fact, the temple would always be at risk without the protection of strong, complete walls.

Nehemiah gives us a clear picture of the relationship between the human spirit (the temple) and the human soul (the walls). Turn for a moment to Appendix A, where you will see simple renderings of Jerusalem before and after the city walls and gates were restored, alongside circle diagrams that represent how human beings are composed.

1. At the core, we have a spirit. It is the relational, worshipful, living center of the human personality.

2. Surrounding the spirit, we have a soul. It is the command center of the human personality, which includes intellect, emotions, and will.

3. Supporting and supported by both spirit and soul, each of us has a body; the body is usually the only part we are familiar with.

So it is the inner workings of our beings that we need to be most concerned with, and we need to know how they function. God's Word distinguishes between the soul and spirit—the "soul me" and the "spirit me." But neither "me" is any less "me" than the other. Both of them need to be formed and enlivened by God's creative and re-creative Spirit.

It is important for us to know this distinction of soul and spirit to best respond to God's work in our personalities. Since the Holy Spirit wants to rebuild all brokenness of soul, it will help to know exactly what goes on there.

DISCERNING BETWEEN SPIRIT, SOUL, AND BODY

The Bible makes a clear distinction between our soul and our spirit (the italics are mine):

1. In 1 Thessalonians 5:23, Paul prayed for the Thessalonians: "Now may the God of peace Himself sanctify you completely; and may your whole *spirit, soul,* and *body* be preserved blameless at the coming of our Lord Jesus Christ."

2. Hebrews 4:12 states, "For the word of God is living and powerful, and sharper than any two-edged sword, piercing even to the division of *soul* and *spirit,* and of joints and marrow, and is a discerner of the thoughts and intents of the heart."

3. In Luke 1:46–47, after Elizabeth had greeted her and confirmed her having conceived the Messiah, Mary sang, "My *soul* magnifies the Lord, and my *spirit* has rejoiced in God my Savior."

The Word not only distinguishes a person's spirit from his or her soul, but it also teaches us the difference between them. It's not for reasons of philosophical argument that God's Word presents the fact that we have three parts to our being. Neither is the tripartite nature some hangover of ancient thought to be replaced today by newer notions. No, God reveals the structure of our being by His Word because He wants to accomplish distinct things in each part of us. He wants us to understand about each part.

The Book of Nehemiah gives us a clear word picture to follow.

The temple, central to the city and central to worship, can be likened to the inner man—the human spirit. Our sin has destroyed our relationship with God and our capacity to worship Him, but rebirth in Christ—like becoming a "reconstructed temple"—makes renewed worship and fellowship with God possible.

The city, central to the rule of the surrounding land or territory, can be likened to the human soul. Just as the walls and gates had been ruined by the punishment for sin, so the human soul—its capacity to live under God's will and rule, to "reign in life" through Jesus Christ (Rom. 5:17)—is marred by sin.

The land in which the city was situated was intended to be a land of peace and fruitful harvest, and it can be likened to the human body. Through it, once He is allowed to redeem and restore, God can channel and manifest His kingdom witness. Interestingly, just as the physical property of the land is dirt—dust—so our bodies are made of dust. (See Genesis 2:7; 3:19.)

The distress of Jerusalem is like our situation before the Holy Spirit comes to restore us. Although we know we've been saved and forgiven, and although we have a sense of the comfort of our Abba, God the Father, still we often feel like failures. We can't conquer certain things. The adversary takes huge delight in causing us to feel the reproach of what "Christians are supposed to be." We are driven to compromise. We feel we need to pretend to be what we have not yet become, and our pretense does nothing to restore what has been broken.

THE FOCUS IS ON THE SOUL

When Nehemiah heard about the condition of the walls, he was dismayed.

> And they said to me, "The survivors who are left from the captivity in the province are there in great distress and reproach. The wall of Jerusalem is also broken down, and its gates are burned with fire." So it was, when I heard these words, that I sat down and wept, and mourned for many days; I was fasting and praying before the God of heaven.
>
> —NEHEMIAH 1:3–4

In Jerusalem, the walls of the city remained broken down long after the temple was restored. Nehemiah knew what he needed to do to remedy that situation, just as the Holy Spirit knows what to do to remedy ours.

The focus of Nehemiah's concern was on the walls, and this relates to the focus of the Holy Spirit's concern, which is on our souls. Here, in Nehemiah's words, is an Old Testament picture of a New Testament truth: "So it was, when I heard these words, that I sat down and wept." Hear the echo of the Holy Spirit's present concern over the activities of some who have been reborn yet remain in a broken-down condition. Their temples have been rebuilt, but their walls have not. The dismay and grief of Nehemiah reflect the very real grief of the Holy Spirit. (See Ephesians 4:30.)

Let me be very direct. Let's sensitize our souls to the issues this study approach surfaces.

Do you see the parallel? Even though our spirit has been reborn (our temple has been restored), we must grow up in Christ, learning to walk no longer with a "darkened understanding," as one who is led by worldly emotions (Eph. 4:17–19).

Nehemiah's tears and the Holy Spirit's grief both center on the unfinished residue of brokenness. Taking their reaction to heart, we need to focus on that part of our being where the rebuilding process is most needed, our soul.

Your soul, like a middleman who determines what of your new life will be translated into new living, sits in the driver's seat. If it is dysfunctional in any way by reason of past habits, pains, or needed repairs, your whole being is affected. Just as broken walls hindered the definition and control of the city, so your saved but unrestored human soul hinders progress.

At the seat of your identity and will, your soul functions as the command center. What goes on there determines the extent to which the King's rule will be manifest in the whole of your being. If there is brokenness or malfunction there, it may not mean your damnation, but it does cause the Holy Spirit consternation.

Your soul includes three essential facets and functions. These essentially comprise your personality:

1. Your intellect—the processes of your intelligence, your mind, your thoughts

2. Your emotions—the processes of your temperament, your feelings, your attitudes

3. Your will—the processes of your choice, your determination, your decisions

Most of what lures, drives, attracts, convinces, persuades, or motivates you is generated at the thought (intellect) or feeling (emotions) level. Affected by this interplay of intellect and emotion is your will, the decision-making center of your soul. The human will is the most awesome feature of your soul—indeed, of your whole being—for it determines *destiny*. By reason of your will, your soul functions as the command center for your whole personality.

What goes on in your soul determines how you feel today (your emotions).

What goes on in your soul determines if you will learn today (with your intellect) those lessons you must know to grow in the understanding of the Lord. Daily decisions determine which feelings you need to respond to or reject in order to obey the will of God, and which attitudes or facts you need to process according to the Holy Spirit's directives. All of this is going on today in your soul. How your mind and emotions interact will generate decisions that either deepen your problems or release your progress.

It is essential to see now the absolute need of your soul being restored. Your reborn spirit may make it possible for you to worship God, but your rebuilt soul will determine your freedom in life, your service for Christ, your fulfillment, peace, and joy.

Action Ahead

Nehemiah's tears preceded his action. It's the same with the Holy Spirit. Far from giving up on you, He is moved with an understanding of your need, and He is ready to bring aid to the site of any weakness in your soul.

The Holy Spirit's actions will address specific areas of brokenness. First, He will evaluate the situation, just as Nehemiah traveled to Jerusalem to see for himself the broken-down walls:

> So I came to Jerusalem and was there three days. Then I arose in the night, I and a few men with me; I told no one what my God had put in my heart to do at Jerusalem; nor was there any animal with me, except the one on which I rode. And I went out by night through the Valley Gate to the Serpent Well and the Refuse Gate, and viewed the walls of Jerusalem which were broken down and its gates which were burned with fire. Then I went on to the Fountain Gate and to the King's Pool, but there was no room for the animal under me to pass. So I went up in the night by the valley, and viewed the wall; then I turned back and entered by the Valley Gate, and so returned. And the officials did not know where I had gone or what I had done; I had not yet told the Jews, the priests, the nobles, the officials, or the others who did the work. Then I said to them, "You see the distress that we are in, how Jerusalem lies waste, and its gates are burned with fire. Come and let us build the wall of Jerusalem, that we may no longer be a reproach."
>
> —Nehemiah 2:11–17

All of us retain emotional residues and scars from childhood experiences, from recent suffering, from disappointments, even when the events themselves seem to have been forgotten. To the soul's emotional wounds are added the mind—a habit here, an insensitivity there, a loss of capacity to respond.

Often what happened to you in early years breeds insecurity. Like a broken wall, no established boundary of identity or secured line of defense exists. "Broken walls" hinder the capacity of the mind to resist unwanted ideas and cripple your emotional strength and ability to be courageous or stable in crises.

Do you seem to be unable to resist temptation? It could be that your soul's crumbled walls and burned gates (destroyed in the battles of your past life) have left you with no line of defense.

Are you easily overcome by doubt or by habit? It could be that your personality is spongy and riddled with holes like shattered walls, providing no security or defense.

Why might you have some physical problems? By reason of your soul's pain, much physical agony may result. Physicians and psychologists attest that physical sickness is often the direct result of mental or emotional upheaval. Our souls (*psyche*) impact our bodies (*soma*), and our physical afflictions are often *psychosomatic*—signs of deeper pain within our personality.

SOME STRAIGHT QUESTIONS

Are there some things going on in your mind that hinder your spiritual growth? Do you feel like those people in the Book of Nehemiah—a reproach and an embarrassment to yourself—so that you feel weakened or crippled in the face of your enemies?

At the mental level, are doubts a real difficulty? How often does your imagination hinder you to the point that it interferes with where you really want to go? How about impure thoughts? How about the inability to focus? Do your thoughts digress to unimportant and insignificant matters? How many times do your reasoning capabilities argue against you rather than work for you? How many times do things going on in your mind torment you, and you find yourself incapable of withstanding them? I'm not talking about a lack in intellect; the issue has nothing to do with your IQ. I am addressing the rubble—the things that don't seem to cooperate with what God is wanting to do and the part that cries out to have the mind of Christ.

And how about the "emotional you"? Do fears surround you? Do lusts clamor for attention, eroding your inner integrity and trying to prompt decisions to feed them? Does anger fester, embittering your attitude toward others? Has unforgiveness lodged deep within, hindering the kind of spiritual growth you'd like to have?

Oh, how these mental and emotional forces work against our will! They cripple our confidence, hinder our attempts to move ahead, and weaken our resistance. It all has to do with a soul needing restoration at points of loss.

Yet, amid all this and deeper still, dear friend, hold on to your core of God-established hope: He has secured the temple within! Your reborn spirit is alive toward Him! His life within you *guarantees* the presence of the heavenly.

NEHEMIAH! THE HELPER IS HERE!

The Lord who saved you has a long-term purpose for you. You will be moved from being marginalized in life to finding the central purpose of your life. Instead of being fractionalized, you will come to know what "holy" really means—"wholly whole," completely restored. So, let me suggest the "you" I've encountered in many who have resonated to the truth we're seeking to grasp here.

First, I am presuming that you're truly earnest about Jesus being your Lord. On those terms, then, let me describe you.

Your spirit (the new you deep inside) loves God unashamedly and unabashedly, and you are owned—totally possessed by Him. You are saved, and you know it. You have that deep, settled confidence: "I am the Lord's." In the past, you might have looked at yourself and said, "If I am the Lord's, why am I like this?" But the answer is now coming into view. You are learning how God's restoration program is included in His gift of redemption in Christ. He regenerated you; He will restore you. Redemption includes a reborn spirit and a restored soul—a certain recovery of all that's been stolen in the past.

The reason the city of Jerusalem hadn't been rebuilt was not because of lack of brains or desire, but it was a matter of opposition and lack of resources. Now Nehemiah had come, bringing with him everything necessary. He would not rebuild the walls by himself but with the active help of the people themselves. Far from rejecting the people or spurning them in disgust because they had not yet fixed the walls (almost a hundred years since the Jews had returned to the city), Nehemiah, like the Holy Spirit Himself, put himself forward to partner with the people.

It's the same with the Holy Spirit. His heart is *for* you. He will make sure that the work happens.

Chapter 4

PARTNERING WITH THE
HOLY SPIRIT IN PRAYER

J OSH BILLINGS, THE AMERICAN humorist, is credited with
saying, "Never work before you eat your breakfast; but if you
ever do have to work before you eat your breakfast, eat your
breakfast first."

Let me play off Billings's counsel and relate it to undertaking the
restoration of the human personality: "Never attempt a spiritual
activity before you pray; but if the circumstance demands activity
before you pray, pray first."

Nehemiah believed in the power of prayer, and, seeing the results
he received, we should too. In the thirteen chapters of the Book of
Nehemiah, there are no less than seventeen prayers.

Most of chapter 1 is one of Nehemiah's intercessory prayers. This
first prayer demonstrates some basic truths concerning the possibilities of effective prayer.

> So it was, when I heard these words, that I sat down and
> wept, and mourned for many days; I was fasting and
> praying before the God of heaven. And I said: "I pray, LORD

God of heaven, O great and awesome God, You who keep Your covenant and mercy with those who love You and observe Your commandments, please let Your ear be attentive and Your eyes open, that You may hear the prayer of Your servant which I pray before You now, day and night, for the children of Israel Your servants, and confess the sins of the children of Israel which we have sinned against You. Both my father's house and I have sinned. We have acted very corruptly against You, and have not kept the commandments, the statutes, nor the ordinances which You commanded Your servant Moses. Remember, I pray, the word that You commanded Your servant Moses, saying, 'If you are unfaithful, I will scatter you among the nations; but if you return to Me, and keep My commandments and do them, though some of you were cast out to the farthest part of the heavens, yet I will gather them from there, and bring them to the place which I have chosen as a dwelling for My name.' Now these are Your servants and Your people, whom You have redeemed by Your great power, and by Your strong hand. O Lord, I pray, please let Your ear be attentive to the prayer of Your servant, and to the prayer of Your servants who desire to fear Your name; and let Your servant prosper this day, I pray, and grant him mercy in the sight of this man."

—Nehemiah 1:4–11

The prayer Nehemiah prayed set the same tone, truth, and thrust of the kind of praying that the Holy Spirit assists believers in. More important, however, is the fact that he prayed at all.

What a wonderful response to an overwhelming situation! Overcome with grief and distress, he could have responded with anger or by becoming depressed. He could have wasted time and energy blaming the king or the people, or even the messenger, Hanani. Instead, with the tears still rolling down his cheeks, he prayed to the only One who was big enough to change the situation.

BEGINNING WITH WORSHIP

> So it was, when I heard these words, that I sat down and wept, and mourned for many days; I was fasting and praying before the God of heaven. And I said: 'I pray, LORD God of heaven, O great and awesome God, You who keep Your covenant and mercy with those who love You and observe Your commandments.
>
> —NEHEMIAH 1:4–5

Nehemiah's opening words express his comprehension of the delicate balance that tunes our hearts with God's. He extols God's greatness and His mercifulness at once and together, viewing His omnipotence and His tenderness simultaneously.

Fully aware of God's grandeur, majesty, and awesomeness, his objective was not to "earn points" or to grovel before the Almighty, nor was it to cultivate a theology. On the contrary, it was to settle his confidence in God's sufficiency to meet his need that Nehemiah praised His greatness. He recognized that God is transcendent beyond all worlds, but that He is also within earshot of the feeblest cry from one of His own. You too can pray this way. God has a "covenant of mercy" with you—just because you love Him.

Commitment to Obey

I pray, Lord God of heaven, O great and awesome God,
You who keep Your covenant and mercy with those who
love You and observe Your commandments…O Lord, I
pray, please let Your ear be attentive to the prayer of Your
servant, and to the prayer of Your servants who desire to
fear Your name.

—Nehemiah 1:5, 11

Notice in this prayer the close relationship between loving God
and obeying Him. The emphasis is on the hearts of those who love
Him and are intent on doing what pleases Him: "Your servants
who desire to fear Your name…who love You and observe Your
commandments." God honors such desire, and your hope and
confidence should rise if you understand the spirit of Nehemiah's
prayer. He had not attained perfection, but he prayed with a heart
of obedience, and God answered him.

I have spoken with thousands of people who view their present
failures as guarantees that God will never be able to complete His
purpose in their lives. For these people—indeed for most of us—a
call to obedience seems a virtual seal against victory, because, they
feel, perfect obedience eludes them. Note again the link this prayer
forges between the heart and the intent to obey. The intent of your
heart to obey the Lord counts far more than what kind of a personality or performance record you possess.

First Samuel 16:7 says, "Man looks at the outward appearance, but
the Lord looks at the heart." Clearly, God is not as concerned with
our perfection as He is with our direction. The praying heart that is

intent on obedience may not immediately perfect those intentions, but God is set to respond to us according to our "heartset."

CONFESSION IN PRAYER

> We have acted very corruptly against You, and have not kept the commandments, the statutes, nor the ordinances which You commanded Your servant Moses.
>
> —NEHEMIAH 1:7

For God's will—rather than our own way—to be realized in our life, we need to be sensitized toward our sin. Only when we confess our sin will the Holy Spirit help us become unchained from the clutching power of past sins and unharnessed from the sin that would seek to find present expression in our lives.

Have you been damaged by sin's impact and are tired of it? Then come confess all that you see as sin and also ask for the insight of the Holy Spirit to perceive whatever sin may still remain.

Awhile back, I found myself feeling uncomfortable about a practice in my own life that I knew to be perfectly and biblically allowable. It involved my television viewing habits. It wasn't as though I was watching impure programming. I wasn't. Nor was it that I was watching television more often than before.

What was at issue, as the Spirit probed my heart, was the fact that I had begun to recognize a new value He was placing on my time. He had been calling me to a deeper sense of responsibility. My privilege was to continue my schedule; His call was to reevaluate it. And the longer I procrastinated, the more I came to see the wasted time as "sin." It wasn't a damning failure, but I was definitely missing something better that God had for me.

As a result, I trimmed my televiewing time (He didn't require me to omit it altogether), and I found real joy in the gain realized through accepting this discipline. First, I had to see my self-indulgence as "sin." The Holy Spirit reproved me for the sin of waste and invited me to confess it. I had taken a pure liberty granted to me as a believer and had turned it into a license for selfishness. It was good to be confronted by the Holy Spirit, and confession in prayer helped me avoid future wasting of time.

THE WORD IN PRAYER

Nehemiah's prayer is grounded in his understanding of the Word of God. He quotes the promises of the Word, and his expressions are drenched in the Spirit of the Word: "Remember, I pray, the word that You commanded Your servant Moses." Then he quotes excerpts from chapter 26 of Leviticus and from Deuteronomy 4 and 28 as well. His affirmations of God's almightiness and awesomeness are more than theological. He is referring to a God who has manifested His power in history. Nehemiah's familiarity with the record of God's workings is at the root of his faith as he prays. He also quotes those portions of the Word that affirm God's lovingkindness and mercy.

Similarly, the Holy Spirit wants to bring the Word of God to our minds as we pray. Praying according to the promises of the Word reminds us that it is God's nature to be good, loving, and merciful. You don't need to be anxious concerning God's will toward you, because He has already revealed His heart toward you: to save, to heal, to rescue, to redeem, to restore, to provide, and to fulfill.

BRING YOUR REQUESTS

"Let Your servant prosper this day" (Neh. 1:11). Nehemiah specifically adds his request for royal favor when he goes to speak with the king about spending a term of duty away from the palace. He is direct in his request, but it is worth noting that his petition comes after he has reviewed the greatness of God in worship and expressed a desire to obey Him, reminded himself and God of his weakness and vulnerability, and remembered how God had helped people in the past, as recorded in the Scriptures.

The rebuilding of your personality begins with humble, faith-filled prayer, and the Holy Spirit will assist you as you pray. Just as Nehemiah came to help the people of Jerusalem, so the Spirit will help our weaknesses when we do not know how to pray as we should. Romans 8:26–27 reads:

> Likewise the Spirit also helps in our weaknesses. For we do not know what we should pray for as we ought, but the Spirit Himself makes intercession for us with groanings which cannot be uttered. Now He who searches the hearts knows what the mind of the Spirit is, because He makes intercession for the saints according to the will of God.

Notice, by the way, that Romans 8:26–27 comes right before the often-quoted verse 28: "We know that all things work together for good to those who love God, to those who are the called according to His purpose." Things do not *always* work together for good automatically. They work together for good only when we partner with God with heartfelt, Spirit-inspired prayer. Did you know that?

There is no greater benefit offered to every believer than the Holy Spirit's assistance in praying "better than we know." The Bible calls this "praying in the Spirit," a privilege He enables by giving us a "prayer language." He does this when we invite Him to fill us completely with His presence and power, and Jesus Himself is ready to pour the Holy Spirit's fullness into us when we ask. (See Acts 2:38–39.)

If you can't think of what to pray, you can always "pray in the Spirit," using your prayer language if you have one. You can count on it—the Holy Spirit is praying for you even when you are not aware of it. The Holy Spirit wants to partner with you in prayer as well as in obedience. The rebuilding process will involve your complete partnership with Him, and prayer is the foundational meeting point for that partnering. We can't do the job without Him, but His power is available to accomplish God's purpose. Daily "executive planning sessions" will advance the project, so schedule your daily session first on your agenda—pray!

As you give your heart to Him in prayer, He will clarify your understanding and give you insight and wisdom. This will be a tangible partnership, and it will highlight God's true heart to you. As you partner with the Holy Spirit in prayer, He will *enable* you in a way that begins to invoke the inflow of the power of God into the situation, often situations that He has not designed at all, but ones in which He desires to work.

But you, beloved, building yourselves up on your most holy faith, praying in the Holy Spirit...Praying always with all prayer and supplication in the Spirit...[who] helps in our weaknesses...[making] intercession for us with [unutterable] groanings...[interceding]...according to the will of God.

—JUDE 20; EPHESIANS 6:18; ROMANS 8:26–27

Chapter 5

WHAT HOLINESS IS REALLY ABOUT

A S OFTEN AS THE word *holy* is used by Christians, you would think that we could all agree on a uniform understanding of its meaning. We read our "Holy Bibles." We receive "holy" Communion. We sing the hymn "Holy, Holy, Holy" and acknowledge the "Holy" Spirit, the third person of the Godhead. We understand the word generally to mean "divine" or "of God."

But when Christians start to discuss "holiness," they discover that the implications of the word vary widely. It seems that holiness can mean anything from a name for the Pope to teetotalism and not wearing makeup.

What do you think it means? What does the word *holy* (or the closely related words *sanctify* or *sanctification*) suggest to you? The word in some form—holy, holiness, holiest, hallow, hallowed—occurs nearly seven hundred times in the English Bible. Certainly, it's an important word.

The average believer seems to feel threatened by the idea of holiness. He tends to see it as something unapproachable, a demanding standard of life that seems to be well beyond him. Believers tend to define it by "feel" more than by fact, and the feeling seems to be, "Boy, that's way beyond me (although I sure want to try my best!)."

WHAT THE HOLY SPIRIT IS UP TO

Our study of Nehemiah's mission—his concern, compassion, and commitment to help the people—is designed to help us understand the Holy Spirit's desire to bring each of us to complete personhood. This practical pursuit—our partnering with Him as He comes to help—is geared to make us whole or holy, That's what "holiness" is really about—wholeness.

What the Holy Spirit is up to is bringing the *whole* life of Jesus Christ into the *whole* of our personalities so that the *whole* love of God can be relayed to the *whole* world.

The word *holy* is derived from the medieval English *hal*, an eleventh-century word that is the root to such contemporary words as *health*, *hale*, *whole*, and *holy*. Obviously, therefore, holiness is more than an esoteric spiritual attribute, and it relates to more than merely the invisible. Holiness involves the completion in all parts of the human being. As the Holy Spirit rebuilds you to the depths of your being...

- Your spirit can be revived to life in God (made holy).

- Your soul can be restored in mind and emotions (made whole).

- Your physical body, habits, and conditions can become disciplined, recovering to well-being (kept healthy).

Now, doesn't holiness look like a far more desirable goal, even a practical, attainable reality? God wants to make us holy, not because He wants churches to be filled with stained-glass people or plaster-cast saints, but because He loves us and wants us to become holy—complete in all our being—just as He is.

Because both terms—holiness and sanctification—have become smothered in religious verbiage and suffocated by programs of legislated standards, we must uncover the truth about holiness if holiness is God's goal for us. If full sanctification is something each of us should truly desire, and if you and I are not likely to hunger or thirst for something that we don't understand or feel intimidated by or have a distorted idea about, we need to explore the real meaning of *holy* some more.

REBUILDING OUR SOULS

In detailing the three-part nature of man (spirit, soul, and body), we earlier read Paul's prayer for the Thessalonian believers:

> Now may the God of peace Himself sanctify you completely; and may your whole spirit, soul, and body be preserved blameless at the coming of our Lord Jesus Christ.
>
> —1 THESSALONIANS 5:23

The words of that prayer reveal three aspects of sanctification or holiness, which is the same as full recovery of spirit, soul, and body:

1. Holiness/sanctification is for *now.*

2. Holiness/sanctification is something *God Himself will do* in you.

3. Holiness/sanctification involves your *peace,
    completeness, and wholeness.*

In short, God is ready to do everything He can to put you fully together, starting today!

This prayer holds a tremendous promise: "May the God of peace...sanctify you." The essential idea of the word *eirene* (peace) is unity, of fragments or separated parts being brought together. This is a wonderful promise, and it is relevant to Jerusalem's broken walls as well as to our own broken hearts. Into both situations has come a strong Comforter, bringing wholeness from brokenness.

Holy as He Is Holy

The phrase "be holy as He is holy," far from being a prohibitive summons or unattainable goal, actually gives us a glimpse into the Father's heart and desire for us.

The phrase is used first in Leviticus: "For I am the LORD your God. You shall therefore consecrate [sanctify] yourselves, and you shall be holy; for I am holy" (Lev. 11:44). It's used again, in essence, in Jesus's words, recorded in Matthew's Gospel: "Therefore you shall be perfect, just as your Father in heaven is perfect" (Matt. 5:48). Here are both an Old Testament and a New Testament summons calling you and me to be *perfect.* How can this be? How can we possibly measure up?

A divine call that was intended to beget hope instead produces fear and condemnation. We will never really gain ground until our sense of being "failures before we start" gets broken.

If the walls of our personalities are going to be rebuilt, each of us will need to come to a place of comfort and confidence about both the goal and the process.

FROM CONDEMNATION TO CONFIDENCE

Nothing hinders the pursuit of holiness more than a sense of condemnation, which always includes guilt, unworthiness, and the sense of impossibility about ever being able to truly measure up to God's standards.

We need to fully "own" the truth that our holiness has been secured before God by virtue of our position in Jesus Christ. In other words, when we received Jesus Christ as our Savior, we were made "positionally" holy. To make it personal for you, that means Jesus's sinless record was credited to your account. The epistle to the Romans often uses the word *justified*, a word indicating that God has made a positive legal judgment about you. By the standards of the highest court in the universe, He regards you as holy when you put your trust in Jesus Christ. He regards you as perfect because Jesus was and is perfect. In Him, we are declared entirely "not guilty" of any sin because the flawless record of Jesus Christ is superimposed over our failures.

God's Word also gets specific about holiness in practice. God wants us to get on with lives that are lived "holily," lives in which we practice holiness in thought and conduct. This implies growth. It's as if we grow up into the positional holiness that Jesus has provided for us. Once we grasp this, we are on the way to understanding "be holy as He is holy" in a new way.

What is the Lord Jesus really saying in the words, "Therefore you shall be perfect, just as your Father in heaven is perfect"? I used to think this was solely a commandment, but I have come to see it as more of a *promise*. Here's what it really means: "Because your Father is holy, you are assured already that you are en route to holiness."

We come to understand two important points: (1) holiness in God's changeless nature, and (2) His promise about our new nature. These understandings bring us to a settled confidence about our future.

Holiness is that attribute of God by which He preserves the integrity of His own being. This means that God never needs to be reminded to be good, loving, wise, or wonderful. He does not say, "I'm going to be nicer today," or "I hope I don't do something evil." He doesn't labor to accomplish that which most of us define as "being holy."

Instead, because God's very nature is holy, He will never be less than what He is already. His holiness guarantees the changeless integrity of His own being.

What does that mean where you are concerned? It means that He will never be without love for you. He will never be less than merciful. He will never be other than just. And He will remake you so that you can reflect His integrity of being in your own personality and actions.

I don't need to tell you that the human personality falls far short of God's integrity of character. Our integrity has been shattered, smashed, and damaged, reduced to far less than it was made to be.

The good news is that we don't have to remain that way. Here comes our Savior! He comes not only to forgive us but also to restore us. His plan is to give birth to each of us all over again and, through this new birth, to place in us a new seed. It's like a new genetic principle: we are to be "born again, not of corruptible seed but incorruptible, through the word of God which lives and abides forever" (1 Pet. 1:23).

We find it hard to believe and even harder to live out. While God's very own Word makes a promise concerning the certainty of this "new seed" potential, our doubts (due to our fears and failures) cause us to live less than whole lives, just as if we dwelt in a city with broken-down walls. The task of rebuilding the walls is too great, so it must be impossible, right? Wrong—the task is indeed great, but "all things are possible to him who believes" (Mark 9:23).

His Seed Will Grow

Whoever abides in Him does not sin. Whoever sins has neither seen Him nor known Him....Whoever has been born of God does not sin, for His seed remains in him; and he cannot sin, because he has been born of God.

—1 John 3:6, 9

I used to read those verses and be ready to give up.

I would say to myself, "Well, I think I'm born of God, but this says that if you are, you don't sin. But sometimes I still do. I don't want to, but I do. I love the Lord, and I'm trying to become more holy, but I still sin."

Then the words of verse 8 would haunt me: "He who sins is of the devil." Doubt and futility would grip me: "Since I'm not sinless yet, am I really saved? So in reality, I must be 'of the devil'?" Years went by, and no one ever told me differently. Like many people, repeated trips to the altar and the prayer room seemed to be the only way I knew to assure God's acceptance. But one day I learned that the same verses that had confused me actually contained a beautiful and mighty truth.

My misunderstanding was overcome simply by discovering the tense of the Greek verb. In this verse, the original language actually says, "Whoever is born of God does not *keep on sinning.*" I had thought it meant, "Whoever is reborn never sins at all, ever again," but it didn't. As a matter of fact, the chapter immediately preceding had already established the idea that it's only by the help of the Spirit of Jesus that we can grow in our ability to resist sin:

> My little children, these things I write to you, so that you may not sin. And if anyone sins, we have an Advocate with the Father, Jesus Christ the righteous. And He Himself is the propitiation for our sins, and not for ours only but also for the whole world.
>
> —1 John 2:1–2

So what the Bible is really saying is this: "Whoever is born of God does not keep on sinning." That is, those of us who have been reborn just don't make good sinners anymore. The more we grow, the harder it gets to keep at it the same way we did before. The message is also this: the seed of His new life in me assures me that my destiny is to conquer sinning. His life in me makes me unhappy when I sin as I did in the past.

How often, before you knew Christ, did you sin and feel justified in doing so? Remember feeling free to retaliate, to let your temper flare, or to serve yourself selfishly? Have you noticed since your rebirth that an inner sense of wanting to please God has begun to predominate? Do you find that you are more sensitive toward doing His will? The reason is this: what is born of God doesn't want to keep on sinning because He has planted His seed in you.

God's seed is in you! He says, "I birthed you into My life, and therefore, the attributes of My personality *will* be forthcoming in you."

BECOMING LIKE FATHER

As any photograph of me reveals, I have a receded hairline. Now, as you can imagine, I did not plan to be balding. In my early twenties I did not make a decision: "I think I'll start losing hair."

But I did begin losing it, and anyone could have predicted that it would happen. Both of my grandfathers and my dad had precisely the same hairline, and the same genetic principle that caused them to be balding was transmitted to me. My brother and I have patterns of baldness similar to our forebears. The biological genetic "seed" that was transmitted to us predestines that this trait will be present in us.

Can you see where I'm going with this?

This rather silly illustration points out how God is saying to you and me, "My seed is in you, and since I am holy, increasingly, you are going to be holy too." We shall be holy for He is holy. We shall become perfected just as our Father in heaven is perfect.

Holiness—His holy nature—is progressively going to fill my broken, weak, and damaged parts. The character and constancy of my Father will grow in me because I am His child.

The Holy Spirit Shows Us the Way

Chapter 1 of the Book of Nehemiah concludes with a calling card that introduces Nehemiah's subsequent conversation with King Artaxerxes: "I was the king's cupbearer."

A cupbearer was much more than a mere servant who handled the king's beverages. The cupbearer in the Persian court was the one who, at times, played a consultant role. The cupbearer was a respected advisor to the crown. This cupbearer status gave Nehemiah his favored access to the emperor, although by no means did it guarantee a favorable response from him.

In the ancient royal court, Artaxerxes, a pagan king, was a monarch who ruled the 127 provinces of the Persian Empire. His empire stretched from the border of China on the east to the Mediterranean on the west, and it included Egypt and Asia Minor. The privilege and power of such a powerful sovereign often manifested itself in impulsive and unpredictable behavior, in acts of passion and outbursts of fury. So when Artaxerxes noticed that Nehemiah's countenance was sad, this was no mere expression of polite concern. Custom required that anyone who came into the king's presence should radiate his sense of privilege. Here was Nehemiah, grief-stricken over the report from Jerusalem, bent and tired from his extended period of fasting with prayer, preoccupied to the point that he was guilty of violating protocol.

"Why the frown?" Artaxerxes demands, noting his cupbearer's gloom.

Nehemiah's response combines three beautiful traits: practical sensitivity, bold assertiveness, and spiritual wisdom. He pacifies the king: "O King, live forever!" (A discreet greeting when there is a distinct possibility of having your head lopped off!) He presents his case: "My forefathers' city is wasted."

And he prays again to God, a brief, pointed, emergency prayer for "grace to help in the time of need." (See Hebrews 4:16.) Then he explains his concern to the king.

Nehemiah explains his desire to oversee a complete reconstruction of the city walls and gates. In explaining the plight of his fellow Jews, Nehemiah's words to King Artaxerxes are neither demeaning nor mocking toward those inhabiting Jerusalem, though long before now the citizens should have launched the task of rebuilding. Instead of faulting the Jerusalemites before the king, Nehemiah shows understanding for them and offers to do everything he can to transform their condition.

Nehemiah said, "Send me, that I may rebuild."

The king replied, "How long will your journey be?"

"And I set him a time." Nehemiah registered his request (Neh. 2:5–6). How long a time did he ask for? As we learn later in the account, Nehemiah asked the king for twelve years!

I can imagine a man asking, "May I have a two-month leave of absence?" or "Well, King, Sire, I would like the opportunity to be there. Could I possibly have a year?"

But twelve years?

Amazingly, the king agrees to Nehemiah's request.

From his reaction at the time he first received Hanani's report of the dire condition of the Jews in Jerusalem, through his willingness to risk his life asking for the king's permission to leave his position, and now to his request for an incredibly long leave of absence—more than a decade—Nehemiah exemplifies the character and heart of the Spirit of God. Nehemiah could not be content until his people were taken care of.

In the same way, the Holy Spirit will not rest until you and I are taken care of. He comes to work in us and with us to rebuild the walls of our God-ordained personalities, and He will not be deterred by the probable length of the task.

And just as the king agreed, so it is today: "The LORD will perfect that which concerns me; Your mercy, O LORD, endures forever" (Ps. 138:8).

Whatever time it takes, He is committed to your completion, and that completed work will be a work of holiness unto the Lord—worked in you by the Holy Spirit of God. The Holy Spirit will complete the job of restoring your personality. He will "reprogram" you.

The Gospel of Matthew reports that as many as touched Jesus were made whole—thoroughly whole (Matt. 14:36). The Gospel of John indicates that a well of the water of new life will bubble up inside you (John 4:14). By the direct action of the Holy Spirit, God will cause that well to burst open so that rivers of the Spirit will flow out of your inner being. That flowing is designed to work a full restoration of the real you.

Let's turn now to the restoration and rebuilding process itself.

Part Two

THE REBUILDING PROCESS BEGINS

Then the king said to me, "What do you request?" So I prayed to the God of heaven. And I said to the king, "If it pleases the king, and if your servant has found favor in your sight, I ask that you send me to Judah, to the city of my fathers' tombs, that I may rebuild it."

Then the king said to me (the queen also sitting beside him), "How long will your journey be? And when will you return?" So it pleased the king to send me; and I set him a time.

Furthermore, I said to the king, "If it pleases the king, let letters be given to me for the governors of the region beyond the River, that they must permit me to pass through till I come to Judah, and a letter to Asaph the keeper of the king's forest, that he must give me timber to make beams for the gates of the citadel which pertains to the temple, for the city wall, and for the house that I will occupy." And the king granted them to me according to the good hand of my God upon me. Then I went to the governors in the region beyond the River, and gave them the king's letters. Now the king had sent captains of the army and horsemen with me....

So I came to Jerusalem and was there three days. Then I arose in the night, I and a few men with me; I told no one what my God had put in my heart to do at Jerusalem; nor was there any animal with me, except the one on which I rode. And I went out by night through the Valley Gate to the Serpent Well and the Refuse Gate, and viewed the walls of Jerusalem which were broken down and its gates which were burned with fire. Then I went on to the Fountain Gate and to the King's Pool, but there was no room for the animal under me to pass. So I went up in the night by the valley, and viewed the wall; then I turned back and entered by the Valley Gate, and so returned. And the officials did not know where I had gone or what I had done; I had not yet told the Jews, the priests, the nobles, the officials, or the others who did the work.

Then I said to them, "You see the distress that we are in, how Jerusalem lies waste, and its gates are burned with fire. Come and let us build the wall of Jerusalem, that we may no longer be a reproach." And I told them of the hand of my God which had been good upon me, and also of the king's words that he had spoken to me. So they said, "Let us rise up and build." Then they set their hands to do this good work. But when Sanballat the Horonite, Tobiah the Ammonite official, and Geshem the Arab heard of it, they laughed at us and despised us, and said, "What is this thing that you are doing? Will you rebel against the king?" So I answered them, and said to them, "The God of heaven Himself will prosper us; therefore we His servants will arise and build, but you have no heritage or right or memorial in Jerusalem."

—NEHEMIAH 2:4–9, 11–20

Chapter 6

RESOURCES AND AUTHORITY

===

OR THE REBUILDING OF your personality, what materials and resources will be required? How will the job be contracted? Are there permits to be issued so that you will comply with the equivalent of city codes?

These are not merely interesting and speculative questions; they are necessary ones. "Rebuilding the real you" is not just a play on words—it's a very real project. It will take real time and will require real materials.

As Nehemiah requested of the king a leave of absence from the court, he took care to collect and plan for the transport of all the resources he would need when he got to Jerusalem, which happened to be over a thousand miles from Shushan (or Susa), the capital city. He also requested the necessary paperwork.

Apparently, God was answering Nehemiah's prayer, since Artaxerxes was as quick to respond favorably to Nehemiah as he was quick to show displeasure over Nehemiah's despondency. The king's demeanor changed immediately, and both he and the queen willingly listened to Nehemiah's numerous and substantial requests.

Nehemiah was prepared. He showed as much forethought and preparedness as we can expect the Holy Spirit to show us.

Nehemiah had seized the opportunity to make his requests known. His specific requests provide us with insight into how we will be provided with specific resources—whatever we may need—for the rebuilding of our personalities.

Here is what Nehemiah requested and received, and here also is how they compare with what you can expect to receive from the King's hand:

1. *Time—an extended period of leave from his duties at the palace.* "All the time that is necessary" is also what the Holy Spirit will spend rebuilding you. He is generous in his patience and mercy.

2. *Authority to enter the region and to traverse the provinces that lay between the capital and Jerusalem.* You too can expect to have all the authority you'll ever need to deal with the considerable "territorial" challenges to your personal rebuilding project.

3. *Physical resources for the actual building project.* In Nehemiah's case, this took the form of timber. Timber was a coveted resource in the dry climate of Judah. In a similar way, the Holy Spirit is pleased to help you lay hold of the principles of life that, like timbers, can provide a framework for the rebuilding process.

4. *A contingent of military troops to secure his mission and support him in the event of opposition.* You can expect the Spirit to provide you with an angelic guard force, and they will stay with you regardless of the length of the journey or the arduousness of the rebuilding process.

In essence, these are the same four resources that you and I need before we can partner with the Holy Spirit to undertake our own personal renewal.

THE NEED FOR LETTERS OF AUTHORITY

Furthermore I said to the king, "If it pleases the king, let letters be given to me for the governors of the region beyond the River, that they must permit me to pass through till I come to Judah."

—NEHEMIAH 2:7

Each of the 127 provinces of the Persian Empire was ruled by a satrap—a provincial governor charged with protecting the emperor's interests and the empire's boundaries. Customs were due, passports were required, documents were checked, and the usual requirements of at least a cursory investigation of all travelers were administered. In Nehemiah's case, an unusual need for evidence of commissioning authority was needed because, upon his arrival in Jerusalem, he would be functioning under a special order of the king's court in order to accomplish his mission. Although his role would not completely displace the regional governor's authority, it would supersede it in many respects. Insofar as the Jews and

Jerusalem were concerned, Nehemiah was invested by Artaxerxes with a higher authority than Sanballat, the satrap over the region. Nehemiah came by the direct authority of the emperor himself. It would greatly expedite his task if he could have complete freedom of passage and if there were no questions as to who was in charge.

Along the same lines, when Jesus ascended to heaven, He expressed at least two promises of far-reaching significance: (1) He would build a church, and (2) He would give the church authority to act in His name (Matt. 16:17–19). He further made clear that the Holy Spirit's coming would provide the power to accomplish the task of building and the ability to exercise the power of His name. Having been born of the Spirit of God, we have been given the power to become sons of God (John 1:12).

Do you see how well Nehemiah exemplifies the Holy Spirit? As participants in His building process, you and I need to understand the authority with which the Holy Spirit endows us. The Comforter wants us all to utilize the "letters of authority" we have been given: "Whatsoever you ask in My name," Jesus said, "the Father will do it for you. All authority has been given to Me in heaven and on Earth." (See John 14:13–14; Matthew 28:18.)

These credentials—the privilege of praying and operating in the name of Jesus—are the letters of authority pressed into your hand by Christ the King. The Holy Spirit will teach you to function in those rights. This is a significant point for you because we are a people living on a planet where authority is contested at every juncture.

Since the Fall, the adversary, like a Persian satrap, is ready to claim authority—unless we can verify higher claim. And we have one! That's exactly what we have been given in Jesus's name. We not only have "throne rights," the right of access to God, but we also have throne rights to advance Christ's kingdom in His name!

Just as Sanballat's authority over Jerusalem and its residents was preempted by Nehemiah's letters (Neh. 2:20), so the Holy Spirit has come to enforce the King's orders concerning you. Whenever the devil seeks to drop a pall of gloom over you, distressing you with a spirit of heaviness, or whenever he seeks to encroach upon the present workings of God's purpose is your life, you can drive him off your property. Tell him, "You have no authority here! In Jesus's name, I declare my right to freedom and the privilege of pursuing God's project in my life."

MATERIALS FOR THE PROJECT

The crucial need for wood for construction projects in ancient days cannot be appreciated by those who operate by today's building standards. We can easily miss the significance of this part of Nehemiah's request, since so many varied construction materials are now utilized in modern construction, and steel is so commonly used for frames and beams in large structures. Nehemiah needed large timbers for the structural framework. They would be absolutely essential for the completion of the project.

> ...and a letter to Asaph the keeper of the king's forest, that he must give me timber to make beams for the gates of the citadel which pertains to the temple, for the city wall, and for the house that I will occupy.
>
> —NEHEMIAH 2:8

Notable, however, is the fact that the vast majority of material needed to constitute the rebuilt walls was already on the site in Jerusalem. The walls would be rebuilt from the broken and charred stones that were already there. The rebuilding effort would use tons of rock, some stones that were still the shape in which they were originally quarried and others that would have been broken beyond apparent use. The important fact is that *all* of the building stones would have to come out of the debris of the former walls.

In the conjoining of these two materials—new beams and old stones—there is another picture of God's redemptive program for restoring broken people like us. First, there are always things that God Himself must bring to our recovery. Paul seems to hint at this supply-line ministry of the Holy Spirit in his letter to the Philippians: "For I know that this will turn out for my deliverance through your prayer and the supply of the Spirit of Jesus Christ.... And My God shall supply all your need..." (Phil. 1:19; 4:19). The Holy Spirit's supply is foreshadowed in Nehemiah's request for those materials that must be brought to the task, those "timbers" of God's resource for renewal that He is more than ready to provide.

There will be also, like the broken, fallen stones of Jerusalem's wall, elements present within you that, though battered by the past, can be readied again for building. There are traits of your own unique personality, memories of your past, qualities of your own character—distinct hallmarks of *you*—that God wants to repair and retain: "For it is God who works in you both to will and to do for His good pleasure" (Phil. 2:13).

These two resources provided by Nehemiah—authority and materials—prefigure the ways God equips us today by the ministry of His Holy Spirit:

1. The new supplies will not be withheld from us, because any adversary will be successfully confronted by our badge of authority: Jesus's name.

2. The task can be approached with always-sufficient resources: a renewable supply of divine grace and a redeeming power to recover building blocks from broken pieces.

Along with all of this, Nehemiah requested and was given a cordon of soldiers, which provides us with another mighty parallel with the ministry of the Holy Spirit to us. The next chapter will tell you what they represent in your rebuilding project.

Chapter 7

ANGELS AND ADVERSARIES

===

MOST OF US CAN point to times when something unexplainable suddenly happened—imminent disaster was averted or remarkable deliverance effected. All of a sudden we recognize it—the Lord has sent help! Sometimes, we become convinced that an angel brought it to us.

Some of the most phenomenal stories I've heard in my life, miraculous stories of invisible but obvious assistance, point to the activity of angels. Intellectuals may taunt those who suggest the possibility of contemporary angelic action, but it isn't fanatical to believe such things occur. We can let the Word open our eyes to see.

Jesus said He could have, at will, summoned a host of angels to rescue Him (Matt. 26:53). The angels He's talking about are neither playful cherubic dolls or sentimentalized "chariot attendants" at death (as in "Swing Low, Sweet Chariot"). He's talking about spiritual beings who are as real as the paper this page is printed on.

There are as many references to angels in the New Testament as in the Old—almost three hundred in all. Even though the Bible has much to say about angels and their role toward us, a dearth of teaching about them exists. There are some people who have so reacted to superstitious ideas about angels that they seem to take exception to confirmed truth on the subject. The religious hangover from medieval traditionalism is not a good reason to disregard the Word.

Of course, other people have become "angel chasers," seeing them everywhere. Paul wrote to the Colossians, "Let no one cheat [defraud] you of your reward, taking delight in false humility and worship of angels" (Col. 2:18). His warning to not become preoccupied with the subject of angels is sound, but it was never intended to remove us from an understanding of their activities.

ANGELS AND YOU

Angels are not merely winged wonders flitting about in the atmosphere. They are "ministering spirits," and they have been appointed to explicit tasks. They have been assigned to minister to "those who will inherit salvation." Hebrews 1:14 asks, rhetorically, "Are they [angels] not all ministering spirits sent forth to minister for those who will inherit salvation?"

Who will inherit salvation? The Bible makes clear who this is: we who are the redeemed in Christ are salvation's heirs. Romans 8:16–17 tells us so: "We are...heirs of God and joint heirs with Christ." In Ephesians 1:11 we read, "In Him [Christ] also we have obtained an inheritance."

Therefore, it is no exaggeration of the Word to accept the fact that included in the vast benefits and promises of the great inheritance God gives us is His provision of the attending ministry of angels. He has sent them—as many as we need—to assist us and to work at His direction on our behalf.

Remember the Acts 12 account of Peter being freed from prison? An angel loosed him from his cell and caused sleep to fall on the guards. (See Acts 12:4–10.)

Remember in Acts 8, when Philip left Samaria to go to the desert to meet a man in need? An angel told him to do that. (See Acts 8:26.)

Remember in Acts 12 when Herod, after he killed James, smugly arrogated authority to himself and suddenly dropped dead under divine judgment? It was an angel who struck him down. (See Acts 12:20–23.)

And remember in Acts 27 when Paul was storm-tossed aboard the ship bound for Rome, and he urged all on board to take heart because God assured him of their safety? An angel delivered that message to him. (See Acts 27:23.)

These are clear New Testament cases of angelic agents assisting people of the kingdom with deliverance, guidance, comfort, and judgment. "Are they not all ministering spirits sent forth to minister for those who will inherit salvation?" (Heb. 1:14). Yes, they are!

Yet you might say, "Those cases are certainly true and quite remarkable, but events like that just don't happen today." But wait a minute—think again. Even if you have not had a firsthand encounter with an angel or you don't happen to know someone who has, the timeless Word of God declares, "For He [the Lord] shall give His angels charge over you, to keep you in all your ways. In their hands they shall bear you up, lest you dash your foot against a stone" (Ps. 91:11–12). We know that angels have the ministry of protecting, and that is at least one of their assignments.

Most of us can only see into the invisible realm with great difficulty. But there is more activity than some suppose. In 2 Kings chapter 6 a marvelous story involving angels is told.

It was during the time of the prophet Elisha, and the king of Syria sent a large military contingent of horses and chariots—a great army—after him. When Elisha's servant saw the enemy surrounding them, he cried out, "Alas, my master! What shall we do?" Elisha's calm response has become a classic quotation: "Do not fear, for those who are with us are more than those who are with them" (2 Kings 6:16).

The wise old prophet not only knew he had divine protection—but he could also see it. When his servant responded by saying, "I don't see any troops on our side," Elisha prayed, "Lord, open his eyes that he may see." And God opened the servant's eyes to see that "the mountain was full of horses and chariots of fire all around Elisha" (v. 17).

This promise is yours as well. God provides accompanying care as well as the protective, the liberating, and the ministering work of angels. He has sent forth angels to minister to us and to act on our behalf.

LIKE AN ARMY ON HORSEBACK

The captains of the army and the horsemen that accompanied Nehemiah beautifully parallel the ministry of angels in the life of the believer. "The king had sent captains of the army and horsemen with me" (Neh. 2:9).

Angels have been assigned to us as the groups were assigned to Nehemiah. Billy Graham, quoting verses 11 and 12 of Psalm 91 ("He shall give His angels charge over you, to keep you in all your ways. In their hands they shall bear you up, lest you dash your foot against a stone.") has said that since the word *angels* occurs there in the plural, he has concluded that there are at least two angels assigned to every believer.

We are like Nehemiah, who came from the king with the appropriate letters of authority and permission to undertake the rebuilding process, but those alone could not have guaranteed that he would be able to make the trip safely or stay long enough under hostile circumstances to complete the task. Success of the wall-rebuilding project was far from being a "given." Nehemiah would face serious opposition. He needed his assigned "angels"—in his case, mounted troops. Their job, like the angels' job for us, is (1) to defend and protect, and (2) to provisionally alter circumstances by their intervention and make things turn out. We have been given angelic "personnel" to serve as a vanguard, a bodyguard, and a rear guard. Let your heart be encouraged—you're not alone.

The contingent of horsemen given to Nehemiah by the king would help him all along the way. Think about it—he had to traverse a thousand miles, crossing many of the 127 provinces of the Persian Empire that stretched across his route. The road was not secure but teeming with outlaws.

This is a great parallel to the widespread opposing forces of the adversary that are "stationed" across our life pathway. Concerted defense was going to be needed by Nehemiah, and it's going to be needed by you and me. Nehemiah faced outlaws, wild beasts, and natural hazards. In essence, so do we. Just as armed troops accompanied Nehemiah from the palace in Shushan, so God, in pouring His Holy Spirit upon the church, has also bequeathed provisionary troops—the hosts of the Lord, bands of angels—to assist us when need arises. We aren't supposed to seek out or worship the angelic guard. God has assigned them to us in our interest, and we can count on their care.

Still, an awareness of hostile forces is important to our understanding. There are dark powers who seek to oppose us. Satan's forces are bent on interfering with what God wants to do in our lives. They definitely do not want you to accomplish God's destiny for your life. The dark powers aligned against us appear in stark contrast to the angelic hosts serving the Father's purpose:

> For we do not wrestle against flesh and blood, but against principalities, against powers, against the rulers of the darkness of this age, against spiritual hosts of wickedness in the heavenly places.
>
> —EPHESIANS 6:12

THE FALLEN ONES

The prophets Isaiah and Ezekiel both speak about the fall of Lucifer. (See Isaiah 14:12–15; Ezekiel 28:11–19.) Under the configuration of the prince of Tyre, Satan is identified as a sinister being, destructive in every design, hideously hateful, and opposed to all that is God's purpose and desire.

In Genesis, he is introduced as the serpent in the garden, the same title that follows him into the Book of Revelation where he is also called the dragon. (See Genesis 3; Revelation 12.) He is referred to primarily as "Satan" (meaning "accuser" and "adversary") and "the devil" (meaning "slanderer"). The Bible reveals that Satan is a spirit being who was originally created in beauty and perfection by the hand and breath of God but who rebelled against the Most High. As a created being, he is finite in his capacities, though he transcends the power of humankind in our present state.

Satan is not omnipotent, however great his power, although he is a formidable adversary. Only God has *all* power. Further, Satan is not omnipresent—only God can be everywhere. Through demon hordes, which, like an evil army, serve at his direction, the devil seeks to strategize and execute his master plan—a program formulated to deceive and destroy individual persons and the whole human race as well.

It is important to know these facts about the devil, for contrary to the notion that he is only an abstract force, a negative way of thought or an impersonal expression of evil, the Bible gives a different picture. God's Word reveals him as a distinct, vile personality who rules the forces of darkness and operates systematically in the spiritual realm against everything good, righteous, noble, pure, and healthy. He commands forces of lesser fallen angels, and he roams throughout the earth.

First Peter 5:8 calls him our "adversary" and teaches us to "be sober, be vigilant; because your adversary the devil walks about like a roaring lion, seeking whom he may devour." Some sincere believers are intimidated by such words and prefer to simply skirt the subject and pretend their enemy will leave them alone if they do the same with him. God's Word says the adversary is *stalking* us. (See 1 Peter 5:8.) If you were being stalked by a lion or another predator, would you just hum and close your eyes, hoping that if you couldn't see or hear your pursuer, he wouldn't attack you?

Let's learn the truth about him so that we can confront him with confidence. How broad is his arena of action? The God we worship and the Christ who redeemed us not only created but also rule the entire universe. Satan's scope of power is only on this planet, Earth. That may be of small comfort, however, since Earth is where we live and his assault seems unavoidable. But before we faint or tremble, remember it is also to this small planet that God has sent His Son and announced, "All authority has been given to Me in heaven and on earth" (Matt. 28:18).

When Jesus offers to us the privilege of being born again into God's kingdom, the fact is that new birth in Him places us outside Satan's realm of rule, even though we continue to live on this planet where the battle still rages for human souls. Perhaps it will help us to grasp the nature of this battle if we understand its history, for people were not originally placed on Earth in this dilemma.

How did Satan gain such powerful rule over this planet? According to the Bible, God created the earth for the governorship of the human race, under God. But through deceit and disobedience, the first people believed the serpent's lie. They listened to the snake, disobeyed their Creator—and handed controlling management of the earth to that serpent, Satan. That management role was originally intended to belong to human beings, who had been created in God's image and inbreathed with His life.

The devil still exercises this rule because he has "just rights," having received license to this rule through man's disobedience to God and his consequent forfeiture of his God-given right to rule.

One way we know the devil has legal claim to function on Earth was evidenced when he offered "all the kingdoms" of this planet to Jesus in an attempt to seduce Him to sin. (See Matthew 4; Mark 1; Luke 4.) Jesus did *not* contest the devil's right to make that offer. Jesus did rebuke the temptation, but He didn't correct the tempter's right to make the proposition.

This is the situation into which we have been born. The struggle goes on. God has won the ultimate victory over Satan's reign of fear and death, and human beings find themselves on both sides. One by one, you and I and others have switched from Satan's side to God's side as we commit our lives to His Son, Jesus.

So, what license does Satan retain to operate in my life and in yours? We know that the entire life of a person outside of Jesus Christ is lived under the sway of the prince of the power of the air, "the spirit who now works in the sons of disobedience" (Eph. 2:2). In other words, an unregenerated person not only is still in his sins because of Adam, but he is also completely vulnerable to the dominion of the adversary by reason of living in his domain.

But this certainly does not mean that every unbeliever is demon-possessed. Nor does it necessarily mean that non-Christians even consciously or willfully serve Satan. What it does mean is that our whole thought system, our whole pattern of life and conduct, is far more motivated, animated, and manipulated by the adversary than we realize. The whole world, the Bible says, is under the influence of the evil one, and that includes us. (See 1 John 5:19.)

How shall we recognize and respond to Satan's workings? There are several telltale traits of his activity:

- The adversary *lies* to people.
- The adversary *imposes fear* on people.
- The adversary *depresses* and *oppresses* people.
- The adversary *sows doubt* in people's minds.
- The adversary seeks to *defeat* and *discourage* people.

Where good things have begun, he will seek to abort what God's Word is doing. When the Word does gain a foothold, he will seek to snatch it away. As your enemy, he will seek to wipe out any and all hope of holy, joyous expectation.

Satan is a liar, but you don't have to respond to the lies of the adversary. He is an oppressor, but you don't have to let him oppress you. We have the Holy Spirit and His angels to help us. Keep Acts 10:38 in mind: "God anointed Jesus of Nazareth with the Holy Spirit and with power [to deliver] ... all who were oppressed by the devil." That's just one of the sure promises we can live in.

Satan also infects hearts and minds with evil. Jesus likened the adversary to a sower of evil seed that grows into a weed-filled garden (Matt. 13:24–30, 36–43), one who directs activity, sowing into your life things that are opposed to God's goodness. He further seeks to steal the good seed of the Word of God when it comes to us. He will attempt to influence you to resist faith-inspiring promises and fruit-bearing seed (see Luke 8:12), but you can counterattack by clinging to and declaring God's Word of truth. Don't let the thief succeed at stealing, killing, or destroying! (See John 10:10.)

James 4:7 declares our authority: "Therefore submit to God. Resist the devil and he will flee from you." Martin Luther wrote regarding Satan's attacks on us: "One little word will *fell* him!"

(That is to say, cast him down and overthrow him as you stand on the promises of God!)

Anything that opposes you has a responding counterforce in God's Word. The Holy Spirit will stir your mind with God's Word to strengthen your heart and secure your faith. Though the thief comes to steal and destroy, the Holy Spirit will rise with Christ's abundance of grace so that your restoration and growth can proceed: "When the enemy comes in like a flood, the Spirit of the LORD will lift up a standard against him" (Isa. 59:19). Victory is yours—now!

Although we live on the scene of this conflict and face these devilish devices, acknowledging the facts about Satan is in no way the same as surrender. You have your rightful place in God's promise and victory. Our Nehemiah—the Holy Spirit—has come with letters of authority that overrule our opponent and preempt his authority over us:

- Truth will overthrow his lies.
- Deliverance will cast out his oppressive works.
- The work of grace will weed out what he seeks to sow.

DEALING WITH THE ADVERSARY

Sanballat's opposition to the efforts on Jerusalem's walls reflect the satanic, tyrannical nature of our adversary, the devil, who is dead set against our wholeness:

When Sanballat the Horonite and Tobiah the Ammonite official heard of it, they were deeply disturbed that a man had come to seek the well-being of the children of Israel.

—NEHEMIAH 2:10

Sanballat was the provincial governor of Samaria, and his control had been absolute. Previously, nothing could happen without his approval. But now, something had overruled that: Nehemiah had brought official letters from the emperor that had put the Jews in Jerusalem under Nehemiah's authority. Appointed as the governor of Judah, his authority superseded that of Sanballat. He had been given the right, if he wished, to annul anything Sanballat decreed.

To think that this spiteful ruler "grieves" that a man has come from the king to help these oppressed and needy people... It is so characteristically satanic!

Sanballat's only interest was to keep the people in a state of defeat and despair, for his sole purpose was to secure his rule over them. He exacted taxes from them, concocted demands of them, and exploited their weaknesses at every turn. He was completely disinterested in the well-being of the people he had been charged by the empire to serve. Sanballat's character is as accurate a picture of Satan as you will find anywhere in Scripture, and his actions—countered by Nehemiah's—provide us with a helpful approach to our own efforts to succeed as the Holy Spirit comes to help us rebuild the walls of our souls.

Just as Nehemiah knew how to deal with Sanballat by leading the Jews in resisting his efforts at hindering them, we need to let the Holy Spirit's message in the Word unmask Satan's person and methods.

PLAYING "AWAY FROM HOME"

Even knowing that God has sent a permanent Helper to guard and guide me, I have at times felt the soul-wearying hostility of hell wearing me down. Amid the struggle, I admit that I have still felt low sometimes, even though I knew I was destined for triumph beyond the test. If you've ever felt like that—wearied though you're winning—maybe this story will help you.

When I played basketball in high school, on one occasion we were playing "away"—playing a game on another school's home court. Our team was playing quite well—outscoring the opposition, in fact—but somehow the sense of winning just wasn't there. Our momentum began to fade. Recognizing the problem, our coach called for a time-out. As we huddled at the sidelines, he began, "Hey, guys, listen up. You're winning. But I know it doesn't 'feel' like it. Now, brace yourselves. Understand this. You're playing on 'enemy territory,' and you've got very little crowd support."

It was true. Because of the distance, very few of the fans from our high school were there. The crowd was made up largely of the fans of our rival team. Every time we scored, we heard nothing but boos. Whatever the other team did was lauded and applauded, and this meant that although we were ahead, a horrible sense of being defeated hung in the air and weighed us down. The coach recognized its effect on us. Having wisely helped us see the source of our "lag," he sent us back into the game with renewed determination. And, of course, we won.

It can sometimes be like that for you in the middle of trying situations. The adversary opposes you. You're in God's will and purpose, yet you feel depressed: "It sure doesn't feel like I'm winning!" But cheer up, teammate!

Don't let the adversary's crowd of demon liars get you down. You may not have the "home court advantage" at this time, but you do have the presence of a Coach who wants you to remember, "He who is in you is greater than he who is in the world" (1 John 4:4).

Yes, Sanballat will continue to prove to be a hatefully accurate picture of Satan. But in Nehemiah, we will further see a strong yet tender picture of the Holy Spirit, confronting evil and advancing the recovery process. In helping you withstand the adversary, the Holy Spirit further assures you:

- "I'm going to get you together..."
- "I'm going to rebuild you..."
- "I'm going to restore you..."
- "...no matter what your adversary tries to throw at you."

Dear one, there's overcoming confidence in perceiving the real nature of the spiritual battle. The enemy and his company are real, but so are the conquering Comforter and His heaven-sent troops.

Everything Satan can do can be overruled by the present ministry of the Holy Spirit in you. Let the Holy Spirit make the letters of authority in God's Word alive to you and in you. Overrule the devil and stand in the certainty that "He who has begun a good work in you will complete it until the day of Jesus Christ" (Phil. 1:6).

You may be uncompleted, but you will never be defeated!

Chapter 8

BREAKING LOOSE FROM CONDEMNATION

O NE OF THE TENDEREST and loveliest verses in the Bible is from the often-quoted Twenty-third Psalm: "He leads me beside the still waters. He restores my soul" (vv. 2–3).

This description of our Savior's faithful, gentle ministry is but another reminder of God's purpose to restore—to recover whatever remains wounded or broken in us. In this regard, the story of Nehemiah provides truth that serves to unmask another obstacle to our fullest development, namely *condemnation.*

Few things are more crushing than condemnation. Its soul-wrenching power can render us mentally and emotionally crippled. Condemnation wipes out one's sense of God's peace and plays havoc with faith's underpinnings.

Jesus, ever our Savior and our soul-restoring Good Shepherd, wants to lead us beside the rivers of Holy Spirit–inspired truth that will liberate us from the shackles of condemnation.

Nehemiah's restoration work in Jerusalem is so representative of the way the Holy Spirit begins His restorative work in us that it's not surprising so many vivid analogies occur.

Before they were destroyed, there were ten gates in the walls of the ancient city of Jerusalem. Nehemiah mentioned visiting the ruins of three of them: the Valley Gate, the Refuse Gate, and the Fountain Gate (Neh. 2:11–15). (See Appendix A for a map of the walls and gates.)

The purpose of this tour, which Nehemiah took before anyone even knew why he had come to Jerusalem, was to evaluate the actual condition of the walls. His survey was to study where he would first need to concentrate his efforts. His report notes that as he proceeded, he finally came to a place where he could go no further. The destruction of years before had been so complete that rubble blocked his passage at every turn. He specified a point on the severe eastward slope where the ruination made it too dangerous to advance any farther. Here, he turned back and reentered the city by way of what remained of the Valley Gate—the point at which he had earlier exited. Nehemiah's survey report gives us both a sense of the devastation at hand and an appreciation for the enormity of the task he faced.

God's Delays Are Not Denials

Out of this study of actual events in history, we discover so many devotional analogies. Types break forth everywhere, picturing redemption and showing how the Holy Spirit works today. As we trace Nehemiah's survey of ruins, notice the phrase "after three days." It's the first of several points at which you'll find parallels quite helpful in breaking free from the enemy's use of condemnation to quench the joy of the Lord in your soul.

Nehemiah's arrival at Jerusalem had been followed by three days of virtual inactivity. There was no fanfare, no high celebration, no announcement of intent, but the Comforter had come—He was on hand to begin work as soon as He was welcomed. The passage of time was doubtless a practical one of adjustment, of his getting settled following the arduous demands of such an extended journey. These three days would also have provided time for thoughtful consideration of his first steps, now that he had actually reached the scene of his mission. But it seems like a long time to do nothing, after such an urgent push to travel from the palace in faraway Shushan.

How often have you wondered why God doesn't do things more quickly? If patience during God's "waiting periods" is trying for even the most mature believer, how much more so is it for those of us still discovering that our receiving of the Holy Spirit rarely includes an immediate change of circumstance?

Over the years I have had many people ask me, "Pastor, since I've been filled with the Holy Spirit, I feel different, but it doesn't seem like much else has changed." They go on to express their concern that a week…two weeks…a month has passed, and yet dramatic events still aren't filling their days "like all those people" they've heard testify.

I usually seek to comfort them with two facts:

1. My experience with dramatic testimonies is that they are honest but usually abbreviated. People report, in condensed version, things that took much

longer to come about. Don't feel like a second-class Christian when time seems to be passing by and action seems slow.

2. God is never in a hurry. Yes, the presence of the Holy Spirit within us does bring an instant witness; He's there and He's at work. (See Romans 8:14.) But remember this: the gifts and the fruit of the Spirit aren't unwrapped with haste or grown at a moment's notice. If things aren't happening fast, that's normal.

The relevance of our learning to recognize that God's delays are not denials is that such understanding can defuse the tendency to feel unworthy (condemned) simply because things aren't happening as quickly as we think they would if we were somehow more acceptable to God.

The simple fact of the matter is that the Lord has quiet times of dealing with our souls. When they come, be of good courage. If you have opened yourself up to the Holy Spirit, be patient. The Holy Spirit knows what He's doing, and a little more time won't make Him falter or fail. God doesn't have to dash about busily in order to prove Himself. He's the One who's in charge, not you. Don't compensate by getting busy yourself, or most likely you will have to undo your work.

Nehemiah makes a triple reference to his nocturnal tour investigating the condition of Jerusalem's walls (Neh. 2:12–13, 15). He was not yet ready to tell the people his plan, nor did he want to reveal his purpose to the provincial government. So under the cover of darkness, silently and quietly, Nehemiah took a small group of men to survey the devastation that had been wrought a century and a half earlier. Even as the people slept, unaware that long-sought help had arrived and that their lifelong humiliation would shortly be overcome, Nehemiah went about his task, dedicated to their interests.

Isn't this just like the Holy Spirit? It is apparent in the Scriptures that God is always awake and alert, tending to our need: "He who keeps Israel [the God of Israel] shall neither slumber nor sleep" (Ps. 121:4). "I lay down and slept; I awoke, for the LORD sustained me" (Ps. 3:5). His Word indicates that even while you are at rest, Father God's program for your blessing is moving forward. As surely as your heart is kept beating through the night, His heart concern for you is being carried out. The darkness is His friend; it is not a cause for concern.

Remember that when darkness surrounds you, even a "dark night of the soul"…when it's so dark that you can't see your hand before your face, spiritually speaking, the Holy Spirit is not idle. He is always doing something. A survey project may be going on. Permit the secret survey work, even when you can't detect it. Don't capitulate to unbelief and doubt and discouragement.

Some time ago, after the passing of a family member, I was moved to do a study on God's activities "in the dark." I was amazed at the number of major events in the Bible in which victory was wrought in the midst of darkness:

- Creation's light burst into the darkness of chaos (Gen. 1).

- Jacob wrestled all night and gained a new identity (Gen. 32).
- Israel's Passover deliverance took place in the night (Exod. 12).
- Gideon's battle unto victory began in midnight hours (Judg. 7).
- Jesus's cross was immersed in a sky of inky blackness though it was midday (Luke 23).

Even when Jesus comes again, it will be as a "thief in the night" (1 Thess. 5:2) and during an era of history predicted as one in which "darkness shall cover the earth, and deep darkness the people" (Isa. 60:2).

This truth can bring brightness and exhilaration to your soul. The Holy Spirit is ministering to your need now. Whatever the apparent darkness, God never forsakes the works of His hands. (See Psalm 138:8.) Rather than allowing the darkness of waiting to become a shadow of doubt, and instead of letting a cloud of questioning deceive you into believing that you are the victim of God's apparent inactivity or unconcern, learn this wisdom: *dark times are intended for your rest.* When they come, lean back and recline in the everlasting arms of the Almighty. Allow the Holy Spirit to work out and through what He's surely doing. I guarantee you that when morning comes, you'll be surprised!

LESSONS AT THE VALLEY GATE

Nehemiah's survey team exited the city precincts at the Valley Gate passageway. This gateway, like all the others, was now only a worn path, no longer a structure. It seems more than coincidental that this is the first point of reference.

Interestingly, the Valley Gate derives its name from its view upon and access to the small, narrow Valley of Hinnom. (See Appendix A.) The Canaanite people had worshiped there long before Nehemiah's visit, far earlier in Jerusalem's history. Human sacrifices had been offered in satanic rituals.

Later in history, at a time when the Hebrew prophets confronted Israel for involving themselves in the same evil rituals, blood and death still stained and shadowed Hinnom. Eventually, when God judged the Jewish people by allowing them to be exiled, the reasons for the judgment included the fact that some had sacrificed their children in this very valley. It had been a shrine of Baal worship, that damning cult that defied God's laws and pled the evil case for perversion. (See Jeremiah 32:35.) Thus the Valley of Hinnom became known as the Valley of the Flame or Fires, a place where human sacrifices had been offered. Even when this period passed, Hinnom still continued to be used as a place for burning rubbish, a fact prompting this valley's adoption as a symbol of the forthcoming horrors of hell. In both the Book of Revelation as well as in Jesus's preaching, an ultimate site of eternal damnation is described as Gehenna (a form of the name Hinnom).

Thus, the Valley Gate's prospect is a ready and logical picture of hell, for it depicts the prospect of a life outside Christ, with neither hope nor meaningful destiny. It is not too far-fetched to observe that one's present life, if outside of God's will, can be "a hell of a life"—hellishly self-centered, hellish in its activity, hellish in its fruit, and hellish in its destiny. What the Valley Gate represented from Israel's past is like what it represents to us; it's the point where the worst of the past is revealed and where it is dealt with conclusively.

That Nehemiah's first survey exits from the Valley Gate parallels the Holy Spirit's desire to start His reconstruction project by begetting in you and me a personal sense of our past having been dealt with. Here is His invitation to us. The Holy Spirit would say, "Stand at the doorway of your life and look on your past. Its future was eternal loss. Just as the Valley Gate faced the western, sunset side of the city, see yourself secured in Christ's forgiveness—the sunset declaring an end to that segment of your life." Standing at Jerusalem's gates, confident that my yesterdays have been concluded, brings a fresh certainty concerning my tomorrows. On the cross Jesus declared, "It is finished!" confirming the completeness of all salvation. Now the Holy Spirit makes it personal: whom the Son sets free is free indeed. (See John 8:36.) You never need to account for the past again.

The Valley Gate indicates the perfect confidence you stand in when you know you are born again and hell is no threat to you. Gehenna is real—you can see the smoke rising and you can smell the stench—but it no longer threatens you. You need a line of demarcation between your past life (Gehenna, the Valley of Hinnom) and your present life. You need a restored wall and a restored Valley Gate.

That's what the Holy Spirit will accomplish in your life. He will establish clear boundaries for you. Once the wall and gates are restored, Satan will be expelled and repelled whenever he tries to reenter.

THE SERPENT WELL

Near the Valley Gate was the Serpent Well. Nehemiah mentioned it, and it is still marked today.

Scholars say the Serpent Well was named in the way folk names have traditionally been ascribed to geographic sites. Just as Native Americans and settlers have given natural features such names as "Devil Mountain" or "Snake Creek" because of specific events that happened there, the Serpent Well was probably named for the fact that a snake had been found and killed there at some time in the distant past.

The image is graphic: At some point, a thirsty man seeking water must have been threatened by a venomous serpent coiled at the well. But he killed the snake and went ahead to slake his thirst. With this picture in our minds, our thirsty souls can hear the words of Jesus, "Whoever drinks of the water that I shall give him will never thirst. But the water...will become...a fountain...springing up into everlasting life" (John 4:14). Yet, just as soon as the serpent (Satan) seeks to prevent access to this joy, the Son of God rises to smite the serpent's head. Now He calls us to drink endlessly at the well of salvation's joy. (See Isaiah 12:3.) As we track with Nehemiah, starting through the Valley Gate and coming to the Serpent Well, we can envision a picture of the Holy Spirit, who wants to bring us to:

- A place of security about our past
- A place of victory over the devil's efforts at depriving us of the daily joy of our salvation

The Holy Spirit would say, "I want to bring you to a well where you will drink with joy and rest without fear, where the serpent is pinned under your feet and under My dominion, which rules in your life. You are no longer subject to the accusations of the liar concerning any aspects of your past sin and failure."

Steadfast confidence in your relationship with God is basic to feeling confident about the future. The Holy Spirit wants to help you with this. If God was sufficient to cover your past, when you were dead in sin and lost from His purpose, He can handle your future now that you are one of His own.

BREAK FREE FROM THE SERPENT

Break free from the serpent's words of condemnation. Whenever the enemy accuses you, learn to resist his efforts by standing in the resources of God's truth. Stand your ground on what God has spoken about your sins:

> If we confess our sins, He is faithful and just to forgive us our sins and to cleanse us from all unrighteousness.
> —1 John 1:9

> As far as the east is from the west, so far has He removed our transgressions from us.
> —Psalm 103:12

> Who is a God like You, pardoning iniquity and passing over the transgression.... [You] will again have compassion on us, and will subdue our iniquities. You will cast all our sins into the depths of the sea.
> —Micah 7:18–19

"Come now, and let us reason together," says the LORD,
"Though your sins are like scarlet, they shall be as white
as snow; though they are red like crimson, they shall be as
wool."

—ISAIAH 1:18

I have blotted out, like a thick cloud, your transgres-
sions, and like a cloud, your sins. Return to Me, for I have
redeemed you.

—ISAIAH 44:22

Then He adds, "Their sins and their lawless deeds I will
remember no more."

—HEBREWS 10:17

That last verse, in which the writer of the letter to the Hebrews
quotes from Jeremiah 31:34, declares one of the mightiest possibilities in the universe: *God forgets sin.* "Their sins and their lawless
deeds I will remember no more." This is not a case of senile forget-
fulness but of divine eradication. He completely removes our sin
record from His memory. In other words, God says, "Because My
sinless Son's record of righteousness is now applied to you, and
because I have no instance of sin to recall about Him, I can't think
of anything you've done that displeases me!"

That's what being justified means. We are acquitted of any
grounds for judgment. We now stand with Christ before the heavenly tribunal, and the Almighty, Father God, Judge of all, says, "I
have superimposed My Son's record over yours. Now I regard you
as never having sinned. Your past is abolished from My memory."

Live in this confidence, loved one. Rejoice in condemnation-free living. No longer afraid of the serpent, you can drink from the well without fear, and you can let it increase in you to the point that it flows out of you like streams of living water. (See John 7:38.)

And the next time the devil comes to remind you about your past, remind him about his future!

Chapter 9

TWO MORE GATES AND A
LIFE-GIVING POOL

CHRISTIANS WONDER, "WHAT'S TAKING so long? How can I get moving? How can I rise above the things that cripple me?" My friend Lane Adams succinctly expressed this feeling in the title of his book *How Come It's Taking Me So Long to Get Better?*

Amazing numbers of believers seek miracles to resolve the problems that cripple their progress. They want Jesus to speak an immediate word: "Rise and walk." Oh, how we all would prefer our growth and rebuilding to be accomplished instantly!

Our Savior responds, "Instead of causing you to walk miraculously, I want to teach you how to walk, step by step. This is My supernaturally natural way."

This process is very much like the natural one by which a child learns to walk. It begins with the child's inborn desire to *want* to get up. He cannot achieve it, but he wants to, so he keeps trying. Eventually he masters the art of standing up. Next he learns to move about while still holding on to something solid. Then, having acquired a healthy sense of balance and confidence, he steps forth on his own, to the joyous delight of the whole family.

There are very real miracles involved in our learning to walk in the life of the Spirit of God, but that doesn't preclude the gradual learning process. We must start with the basics and watch for occasional miracles. First steps may be slow in coming, but that makes the miracles even more joyful than they would be if we experienced nothing but a continuum of phenomenal events.

First Steps

When our oldest son, Jack Jr., was born, his feet pointed almost directly outward. At first we thought this would gradually remedy itself. But by the time he began scrambling around and pulling himself to his feet, nothing had changed. As Jack began to walk, it was with difficulty. This gave us sufficient cause to take him to the doctor for examination and treatment. He was fitted with special shoes that he wore for months, but still no improvement occurred. It appeared that the next thing would be to put our son into leg braces.

What follows is one of the most precious stories in our family history, and my wife Anna tells it best. She had just left one doctor's office for another. The first, who had been caring for little Jack, had recommended that he be fitted with braces and given therapy by an advanced specialist. Anna had just boarded the bus en route to an appointment with another specialist that morning, and, with our son in her lap and her hands grasping his feet, she simply prayed, "Lord Jesus, You know how much I would like this little boy's feet to be all right." That was the entire prayer! Minutes later, as she disembarked from the bus and entered the next specialist's office, they both looked with astonishment at Jack's feet—they were perfectly straight! What months in remedial shoes had not changed had been rectified by the touch of Jesus in a mere fifteen minutes! They were both dumbfounded with delight, and you can imagine the praise session Anna and I had together as we laughed and rejoiced over the genuine miracle of the instant recovery of our little boy's condition.

We still rejoice when relating that episode. It was real; we did not imagine it, and it was given by God's grace. I tell it here because there is within it a principle about our learning to walk in the Spirit. Young believers, like young children, do have the capacity to stand, the ability to get around, and the desire to move forward with balance. But there remains a miraculous dimension of life into which we all need to move forward if we are to run the race of a Spirit-filled life.

"First steps," including the miracle of a life-giving water supply, also appear in the account of Nehemiah. In the last chapter, we examined two of those steps, represented by the Valley Gate and the Serpent's Well. In this chapter, we will look at three more stops on Nehemiah's excursion. These next steps depict further foundational points of moving forward in a Spirit-filled walk.

DEALING WITH SIN—THE REFUSE GATE

In verse 13 of chapter 2, Nehemiah says, "And I went out by night through…the Refuse Gate." In older translations, the Refuse Gate was called the "Dung Gate," a name it bears to this day in modern Israel. Naming a portal after the word for excrement seems unusual and distasteful. But the fact is that daily, the city's garbage was removed through this gate, and that refuse included human and animal excrement. Obviously then, the Refuse Gate is a picture of the purging and cleansing process that every believer walks through daily.

There is nothing more fundamental to a healthy walk with Christ than this daily process. As completely as our past sins have been forgiven and our position as sons of God has been secured through our Father's grace, there is still a need for maintaining our hearts in purity before Him. The Refuse Gate was among the first few places scrutinized by Nehemiah, and this reflects the Holy Spirit's desire to keep us sensitive to sin, obedient in our motives and actions, and conscientious to confess our sin when we fail. "But if we walk in the light as He is in the light, we have fellowship with one another, and the blood of Jesus Christ His Son cleanses us from all sin" (1 John 1:7).

It can be difficult to talk with people about their own need for keeping sensitive to confess their sin and be cleansed of it daily. Too many individuals are quick to resist, feeling condemned instead of helped. It seems as soon as they hear anything about their sinfulness, they automatically press a giant "self-destruct" button in their souls, and condemnation clouds their faces. However, if they can learn to bypass the condemnation detour, they will be on a faster track to holiness of life. Jesus Christ does not point out your sin to condemn you; He reveals it so you will confess, repent, and enter into a new level of freedom. We are meant to dwell in the light. You will find cleansing, confidence, and joy every day as the blood of Jesus Christ delivers and purifies you.

This daily need for confession is similar to your body's breathing process. As you inhale, life-giving oxygen is carried to your bloodstream and courses throughout your whole body. As it circulates, your blood picks up impurities and refuse from your cells, and the waste matter is collected and expelled from your body. Similarly, as you daily "breathe" in the life-giving Word of God, the Holy Spirit collects the impurities of your sin and, by your confession and the power of the blood of Jesus Christ, cleanses and purifies your soul.

When the Holy Spirit brings your sin to the surface, it is not with an accusing, "Aha, I caught you!" as though some heavenly helicopter were spotlighting your failure until the angelic cops arrive! He simply uses the light of the Word to show you what He wants to deal with next in your life.

When sin surfaces, confession is required: "If we confess our sins, He is faithful and just to forgive us our sins and to cleanse us from all unrighteousness" (1 John 1:9). The combination of the Word, confession, and the blood of Jesus Christ will work their way through your spiritual system, beginning to purify everything as you allow it to do so.

The Greek word for "confession" is *homologeo*. It means, "to speak the same thing." So when you confess, you say about your sin whatever God is saying to you about it. You agree with His assessment. Confession involves being honest, forthright, and not excusing yourself either to God or to your own conscience. If the Father says, "I don't want you to do that," you respond, "Lord, You're right. I don't want to do that anymore." If He says, "I see that you have not yet surrendered that," then say, "I see it now, Lord, and I do surrender it." When you say the same thing that He says (confession), the light of His Word, along with the cleansing power of the blood of Christ, progressively purifies you.

This is practical sanctification. It does not threaten the position you have gained in Christ. Your assurance in Him is not sacrificed during this process of daily cleansing and empowering, but rather you are moving forward into holiness—that is, the restoration of the wholeness of your personality.

Remember—it's a *relationship*. With a childlike openness, you can walk hand in hand with the Lord in simple, humble adherence to the way He leads you on. Whether or not you can list sins by name, you can expect the cleansing to occur as long as you stay close to Him.

You can't be any more accepted than you already are as His child. You can't be any more victorious than you are in the dominion He has given you over the power of the enemy. But you can become progressively more open to His victory in the practical details of daily living by allowing the Holy Spirit's purifying process to take place on a regular basis in your life.

The Dung Gate is part of the program. It's nothing to be ashamed of; it's healthy.

Being in the Word—the Fountain Gate

After exiting through the Valley Gate and viewing the remains of the Dung (Refuse) Gate, Nehemiah came around to the Fountain Gate. Most scholars believe that the Fountain Gate was given its name because its eastward location was just above and opened to a path leading down to the Kidron Brook, which runs through the Kidron Valley. (See Appendix A.) It would have been the gate through which many of the people went daily in order to get fresh water.

The Fountain Gate depicts the Word of God, which is described as bread, milk, gold, honey, a mirror, a hammer—and, in John 15, as water. (See John 15:3.) Just as the people needed to obtain fresh, life-sustaining water by passing through the Fountain Gate every day, so a believer needs a continuous stream of the Word of God in order to survive.

BEING FULL OF THE HOLY SPIRIT—THE KING'S POOL

Near the Fountain Gate was the King's Pool, which had been created approximately three hundred years before Nehemiah's time. In about 750 B.C., Hezekiah, one of Judah's godly kings, rose to power. Among his building projects was the carving of a strategic underground conduit, which was designed to bring a fresh water supply right into the city of Jerusalem. Until that time, whenever Jerusalem was attacked by enemies, a simple siege could cut them off from the water outside the walls and reduce the people to defeat. But now, thanks to Hezekiah, the solid granite conduit brought water from the Gihon Spring outside the city walls to a pool built within the city (later named the King's Pool). It was a remarkable engineering accomplishment for any time, but all the more considering the conduit was dug more than twenty-seven hundred years ago! Archeologists have found that the workers started from opposite ends and cut their way through the rock to within one foot of a precise contact.

When the King's Pool was dedicated, it meant that a continual, life-sustaining water supply was now within the city of Jerusalem. This was a flowing pool, not a well or a cistern. Some scholars suggest that Psalm 46 was penned to be sung at the celebration of that pool's inaugural: "There is a river whose streams shall make glad the city of God" (v. 4).

The King's Pool was functional in Jesus's time (and still is today), and by then it was called the Pool of Siloam. Remember when Jesus put mud on the blind man's eyes? He said, "Go, wash in the pool of Siloam," and the man born blind could see for the first time in his life (John 9:7).

The King's Pool provides the picture of supply, a flow of living water within us that:

- Helps us to resist attack
- Sustains and refreshes life
- Ministers healing

What a beautiful portrayal of the life of a believer—filled with the Holy Spirit! With ever-fresh supply, the Spirit dwelling in you keeps you alive in Christ even when enemies lay siege to you, refreshing you and sustaining you, cleansing you and healing you from one day to the next.

At the Valley Gate and the Serpent Well, you learn confident assurance in Christ and dominion over the adversary. At the Dung and Fountain Gates, you are reminded of the importance of confession and the daily growth that comes through the Word of God.

Now, if you haven't yet done it, allow the Lord to open in you a conduit of His Holy Spirit, an ever-flowing stream of living water. This fulfills His promise, which is to you personally as much as it is to every other believer in the body of Christ: "You shall receive the gift of the Holy Spirit" (Acts 2:38).

To His promise of salvation's "fountain of water springing up into everlasting life" (John 4:14), Jesus has added the offer of His Spirit's "rivers of living water" (John 7:38) flowing from within you.

Jesus wants you to be filled with the Holy Spirit. Here is a miracle resource of power, flowing from an unending source. "Spirit-fullness" can strengthen you when you're under attack, provide refreshment through daily prayer and praise, and release a flow of Christ's ministering, healing power in you and through you to others.

Ask Jesus to fill you with the Holy Spirit. With praise in your heart and on your lips, come into His presence, and, by faith, receive His promise because "the promise is to you" (Acts 2:39). Expect His miraculous touch upon you as He answers your invitation.

Continue daily in a fresh walk in Holy Spirit-fullness. Ephesians 5:18 literally reads, "[Keep on being] filled with the Spirit." You cannot be sustained by drinking only once. But having been satisfied initially, keep coming daily to King Jesus's pool, the Holy Spirit's never-ending fountain of living water.

Then you can become an overflow to others!

THREE GATES, TWO WATER SOURCES

To review: just as Nehemiah examined the condition of three gates on the southeast side of the city, as well as the condition of two sources of water, so too do each of us need to retrace his steps in order to move forward in our walk with God.

- With a view of the consequences of sin, you need to know where you stand with God in Christ (the Valley Gate).
- You need to remember that you have been given dominion over the devil in Jesus's name (the Serpent Well).
- You need to practice the regular confession of sin to allow an ongoing, purifying work of the Holy Spirit (the Dung Gate).
- You need to drink from the Word of God daily (the Fountain Gate).
- Last but certainly not least, you need to know what it means to be filled with and live in the fullness of the Spirit (the King's Pool)—right on the inside of your being.

Chapter 10

INVITATION TO BUILD

AFTER THE THREE DAYS, Nehemiah gathered the Jews, the priests, the nobles, and the officials to tell them why he had come and to rally them to the wall-building cause.

This was the first time any of them had heard about it. While they had known that a visitor had arrived from Shushan, and while some of them had learned his name and the fact that he was a respected officer in Artaxerxes's court, nobody had discovered his reason for coming or his intent. They knew nothing of his midnight survey, and they did not yet know the authority with which he had been endowed to accomplish the daunting task of rebuilding the walls of their city.

Hear his first words: "You see the distress that we are in.... Come and let us build... that we may no longer be a reproach" (Neh. 2:17). Nehemiah's magnanimous approach demonstrates his complete identification with the people. He includes himself in their predicament. The remarkable sensitivity and gentleness shown by Nehemiah must have been the reason why he elicited such trust and cooperation from the people.

Another scenario might have taken place if Nehemiah, with his exalted, high court position, had come to the people with a self-important attitude. Perhaps his greeting would have sounded more like this:

"I bring you greetings from the emperor's palace where I hold the position of cupbearer." [He pauses and issues a condescending smile. Then he continues, with mild disdain.]

"It is somewhat awkward for me to have to say this, but the fact is, I have come out of sheer frustration with the endless reports we receive in Shushan that you people have not been able to get this city into reasonable and respectable order. You people don't have walls; you have rubble!

"As a self-respecting and concerned Jew myself, I have come to see to it that something is done about the embarrassing state of affairs here, which is inexcusable. The gates are in the same burned condition as when Nebuchadnezzar left the city one hundred fifty years ago. All the Jews in Persia are perturbed. After all, what takes place here in Jerusalem reflects on Jews everywhere.

"I hope you can appreciate the sacrifice and inconvenience I have endured to make this trip to provide you with some leadership. I've brought orders from Artaxerxes mandating your cooperation. Naturally, I'm hoping I won't have to apply the power of my office, but my letters from the king allow me considerable authority should I need it.

"Your obvious lack of initiative with regard to the walls is a concern to me. I hope you will recognize that my time is important, and the opportunity and the benefit are entirely yours. I don't need this work, and I might well have remained in Shushan. But in the hope that my patriotism and good will toward you and the project will bring out the best in you people, I am now ready to begin. I'll be issuing orders later this week and will expect work teams to be on time. If I can get what I expect out of you, I'll have this project sewed up in reasonably short order and be able to get back to Persia.

"Am I understood?"

This may sound like cheap melodrama, but it is not hard to imagine. Yet Nehemiah did not present himself in a pretentious manner, nor did he need to lord it over the people. Like Jesus, he came to set at liberty those who were oppressed, so vulnerable they were like open prey. (See Luke 4:18.)

In the area of our minds and emotions, we are so often like open prey, defenseless. The walls of our souls are still rubble, and we have to scramble to defend ourselves from enemy incursions.

We have been plagued for so long that we can hardly believe our ears when the Holy Spirit invites us to participate in a reconstruction project. This is like a dream come true, a new beginning! Hope is reborn in our hearts. No longer will we have to cower under threatening circumstances. The invitation alone is enough to restore us to strength and resolve.

FEELING GOOD ABOUT YOURSELF

We hear a great deal of talk about "how you feel about yourself"—and with good reason. There are so many forces in our world today that reduce one's self-esteem that it's hard for people *not* to feel worthless, insignificant, and negative about themselves, no matter what their status.

People attempt to counter their own low self-esteem by mounting a self-improvement campaign. They may purport to help you with your low self-esteem by selling you a self-help program. Whatever your perceived need, you can find someone who is eager to show you how to feel better by improving your physique, learning new skills, striking it rich, rejuvenating your sex life, or learning how to resolve tension or other psychological issues. All you need is a new therapist, a new broker, a new "life coach," a new suit of clothes, a new spouse, a different career, a late-model car, a new house, a fresh hairstyle, better vitamins, or another credit card.

As I'm sure you know, "new and improved" vanity is not the same as identity. Far more than "validation," people need genuine deliverance, healing, restoration, and reinforcement. But human resources, however sincerely motivated or professionally administered, can never effect a completely satisfying transformation.

"You have made us for Yourself," Augustine wrote of God, "and our souls find no rest until they find it in You."

Nehemiah's sensitive approach toward assisting the people of Jerusalem is important for more than diplomatic reasons. Humanly speaking, he will have a much better chance at gaining the people's trust and ensuring strong work relations by treating them with respect. He wasn't putting on a performance to win them over. His words and behavior revealed a true, deep-seated sense of identification with those he had come to help.

Here is a man who surrendered high position at the world capital; prepared extensively to supply a multiple-year-long project; endured a demanding trip, escorted by royal troops; and yet, upon his arrival, demanded no honor or deference from the Jerusalem elders. Instead, he simply identified with their plight. He became one with them.

In this same way, the almighty God seeks to redeem each of us. He stoops low. He comes as the incarnate Jesus, lays down His life, and then sends His Spirit to help, heal, strengthen, and rebuild the personalities of those He has redeemed.

The most humbling fact revealed in the Bible is not our guilt before God because of our sin, but that the God who made us and whom we disobeyed has chosen to love us rather than condemn us. An honest look at our muddle—whether we look at our personal lives or at the condition of the entire human race—is sufficient to justify God's saying, had He chosen to do so, "I'm tired of these ungrateful people," and leave us to our own destruction. Remarkably, instead, His own Word tells us that, "God so loved the world that He gave His only begotten Son, that whoever believes in Him should not perish but have everlasting life. For God did not send His Son into the world to condemn the world, but that the world through Him might be saved" (John 3:16–17).

The whole program of God's redemption is one of a loving identification with His subjects—that's us. Understanding this incredible reality is the only way anyone can learn how to feel good about themselves. Not only does God love and reach to me, but also He is not ashamed to completely identify with me. Now I have discovered a foundation for rebuilding the broken walls of my soul.

Nehemiah's words point out three things characterizing the Holy Spirit's mission to rebuild us:

1. He is *compassionate* toward us.

2. He is *committed* to help us.

3. He wants to be our *companion*.

Compassion: "Look at the distress we are in." The words pulsate with understanding. They seem to say, "Your pain is my pain. I don't see you as a problem; I see the problem as ours."

Commitment: "Let us rise up and build." The invitation is to partnership, not servitude. The heart of God is revealed as being fully set on ennobling us, the fallen ones. His redemption is designed to restore us as joint heirs with Him. (See Romans 8:17.)

Companionship: "That we no longer be a reproach." What? Is Nehemiah including himself as a reproach? Nehemiah had nothing to be ashamed of, and neither has God. Still He comes to companion so completely with His beloved creature, man, that His Holy Spirit would breathe to our hearts, "You were made in His image, and until it's restored, He considers your incompleteness a reduction of His purpose. He will not rest until His character is vindicated by its fullest, most beautiful recovery in you."

It is clearly God's desire to restore the whole of you, and biblical grounds for "feeling better about yourself" far surpass mere psychological ones.

Not Everybody Is Happy About It

So it was that the people took heart at Nehemiah's words. "They said, 'Let us rise up and build.' Then they set their hands to this good work" (Neh. 2:18).

Just as soon as they did so, however, they were immediately beset by their opponents: "But when Sanballat the Horonite, Tobiah the Ammonite official, and Geshem the Arab heard of it, they laughed at us and despised us, and said, 'What is this thing that you are doing? Will you rebel against the king?'" (v. 19).

This mocking confrontation portrays the predictable—often vicious—satanic opposition that will always be hurled at you just when your hope has begun to rise. As soon as faith comes—"God is really going to work something beautiful in my life"—and you respond, willing to partner with His purpose, you can count on it: Sanballat—the accuser, Satan—will dig in: "You have no right to even think of that! Are you about to rebel against the king?" This is a classic tactic of the adversary: intimidation in the guise of God's holiness: "Wait!" the enemy shrills at you. "Don't you realize your past life has removed your right to future fulfillment? You've rebelled against God's holy standards, and now you think you deserve His blessing? No way!"

But we have an advocate in heaven—Jesus Christ, and His Holy Spirit will stand beside you, identifying with you, and confront the enemy of your soul just as Nehemiah did on behalf of the people of Jerusalem. To Sanballat, Nehemiah declared, "The God of heaven Himself will prosper us; therefore we His servants will arise and build, but you have no heritage or right or memorial in Jerusalem" (v. 20).

God assures us that He will prosper our efforts and restore our lives because He has declared in His Word that He is for us: "If God is for us, who can be against us? . . . Who shall bring a charge against God's elect? It is God who justifies. Who is he who condemns?" (Rom. 8:31–34).

Nehemiah crushed Sanballat's case with the words, "You have no heritage or right or memorial in Jerusalem," and his adversary's claim was removed. It can be the same with you. Receive the Comforter's declaration, and rejoice in this knowledge: You belong to the Lord. He is totally committed to your fulfillment, and He has willed the completion of His created purpose in your life.

Sometimes, we are up against opposition that is rooted in history, which makes it not our fault in the least. Most of it, however, is outright vicious assault. Just as Nehemiah had to confront Sanballat, Tobiah, and Geshem, so we have to confront:

- Satanic attacks (Sanballat)
- The weakness of our own flesh and our susceptibility to temptation (Tobiah—who was a turncoat Jew)
- The circumstantial difficulties that seem to conspire against us (like Geshem)

We hear the enemy's taunting voice whenever we have a God-given dream. We hear, "Who do you think you are? You can't do that!" Too often in such moments, we allow ourselves to be defeated by listening to the devil's interpretation of our circumstances. It's as if Satan says, "Heel," and we obey him. People traipse around, heeling to the devil's negation of their God-given identity.

The devil knows he can't get us back from Jesus, but he'll use doubt, intimidation, mockery, and oppression to keep us from listening to the Holy Spirit.

IRRITATED WITH JESUS

Jesus knows what it's like. Religious leaders were constantly irritated with Him. His teaching raised their hackles time and again as He confronted their empty notions about God. One of the things they were most aggravated about was His receptivity toward people whom the religionists rejected as unworthy. "Then all the tax collectors and the sinners drew near to hear Him...and the Pharisees and scribes murmured, saying, 'This man receives sinners'" (Luke 15:1–2). Following this incident, as if to add the last straw, Jesus had dinner with a group of "rejects."

The enemy was (and is) irritated to the point of murderous rage, but we can take heart, realizing that while the religionists might turn us away, our Savior will not abandon us.

Jesus taught three consecutive parables to show us God's heart and to give us a clear picture of how God feels about you and me. First, He told the parable of the lost sheep (Luke 15:4–7). His message was clear: not one person is unimportant to God, even though we're but one among the multitudes of humanity.

In the second parable, Jesus described a woman who had lost a valuable coin (Luke 15:8–10). Then she found it again. Bursting with joy, she wanted everyone to know about it. In this parable, Jesus shows us God's heart, as if to say, "Since you want Me as much as I want you, be assured—we will rejoice together in finding and fulfilling your deepest longings, because they represent what I have placed in you."

The third parable, the story of the prodigal son, is one of Jesus's most magnificent ones. (Read it in Luke 15:11–32.) God's heart is completely unveiled in the story of a father who receives with rejoicing and love the return of his son after he has engaged in rebellious, riotous behavior. It is a picture of God reaching out openly to the most miserable failure who is willing to return to Him. In light of that story of consummate waste and ruined potential, ask yourself the question: "How does God—Father, Son, and Holy Spirit—feel about me, my failures, and my waste of divinely provided opportunities?" Jesus's teaching gives an unmistakable answer: You're worth everything to Him! Your failures have not removed your possibilities.

NEHEMIAH/HOLY SPIRIT

Nehemiah said, "I told them of the hand of my God which had been good upon me, and also of the king's words that he had spoken to me" (Neh. 2:18). In the same way, the Holy Spirit wants to assure you now. God's "good hand"—His pleasure to receive you and to help you to rebuild the broken pieces of your life—is upon you. The words of His invitation to rebuild are still hanging in the air. What will you say to Him?

Part Three

REBUILDING TO LAST

Then Eliashib the high priest rose up with his brethren the priests and built the Sheep Gate; they consecrated it and hung its doors. They built as far as the Tower of the Hundred, and consecrated it, then as far as the Tower of Hananel. Next to Eliashib the men of Jericho built. And next to them Zaccur...

Also the sons of Hassenaah built the Fish Gate; they laid its beams and hung its doors with its bolts and bars. And next to them Meremoth...

Moreover Jehoiada...repaired the Old Gate...And next to him was Shallum the son of Hallohesh, leader of half the district of Jerusalem; he and his daughters made repairs. Hanun and the inhabitants of Zanoah repaired the Valley Gate....Malchijah...repaired the Refuse Gate; he built it and hung its doors with its bolts and bars. Shallun...leader of the district of Mizpah, repaired the Fountain Gate....Moreover the Nethinim who dwelt in Ophel made repairs...of the Water Gate....Beyond the Horse Gate the priests made repairs....After them Zadok...made repairs in front of his own house. After him Shemaiah the son of Shechaniah, the keeper of the East Gate, made repairs....After him Malchijah, one of the goldsmiths, made repairs as far as the house of the Nethinim and of the merchants, in front of the Miphkad Gate, and as far as the upper room at the corner. And between the upper room at the corner, as far as the Sheep Gate, the goldsmiths and the merchants made repairs.

But it so happened, when Sanballat heard that we were rebuilding the wall, that he was furious and very indignant, and mocked the Jews. And he spoke before his brethren and the army of Samaria, and said, "What are these feeble Jews doing? Will they fortify themselves? Will they offer sacrifices? Will they complete it in a day? Will they revive the stones from the heaps of rubbish—stones that are burned?"...

Now it happened, when Sanballat, Tobiah, the Arabs, the Ammonites, and the Ashdodites heard that the walls of Jerusalem were being restored and the gaps were beginning to be closed, that they became very angry, and all of them conspired together to come and attack Jerusalem and create confusion....

And our adversaries said, "They will neither know nor see anything, till we come into their midst and kill them and cause the work to cease."...

Therefore I positioned men behind the lower parts of the wall, at the openings; and I set the people according to their families, with their swords, their spears, and their bows. And I looked, and arose and said to the nobles, to the leaders, and to the rest of the people, "Do not be afraid of them. Remember the Lord, great and awesome, and fight for your brethren, your sons, your daughters, your wives, and your houses."

...So it was, from that time on, that half of my servants worked at construction, while the other half held the spears, the shields, the bows, and wore armor; and the leaders were behind all the house of Judah. Those who built on the wall, and those who carried burdens, loaded themselves so that with one hand they worked at construction, and with the other held a weapon. Every one of the builders had his sword girded at his side as he built.

—NEHEMIAH 3:1–32; 4:1–18

Chapter 11

PEOPLE WHO NEED PEOPLE

═══════════════════════

HARD-TO-PRONOUNCE NAME LISTS CONSTITUTE whole chapters of the Bible and make for difficult and boring reading. Nehemiah 3 is such a chapter. I was about to skip it, thinking it had no application to my study of Nehemiah, until I was reminded of a lesson I learned long ago when I was struggling through another name list—the first chapter of Matthew. I remember thinking at that time, "What a strange and uninviting way to begin the New Testament." But then it occurred to me that God must have had a reason for including it, so I paused to inquire of the Lord, asking Him to provide me with an understanding about it. As I prayed, the Holy Spirit helped me to see at least three reasons God puts name lists in His Word:

1. He cares about and remembers people, individually and by name.

2. He makes and keeps promises to people.

3. He accomplishes His purpose in people and through people, not alone by Himself, and not with people in isolation from each other.

So God made sure that we have a record of the names of the people who were key players in the rebuilding of Jerusalem's walls.

The Lord puts great emphasis on the individual. He knows you and me by name. He puts importance on our personalities. These names listed in Nehemiah were real people, just as you and I are real people. We aren't dealing here with the guards who came from Shushan with Nehemiah, who represent the angels in our lives. In this list of names, we are dealing with real people, fellow sufferers from the human condition. We are dealing with fellow builders.

WE NEED EACH OTHER

Rebuilding those walls was a task of overwhelming size and complexity; the perimeter of the walls was more than two miles around. Nehemiah 3 describes how the sweeping project of reconstructing the walls was organized.

Reconstruction of each specific section of the wall, and each of the ten gate sites, was assigned to large family groups or to the inhabitants of smaller villages that surrounded Jerusalem. These people were formed into teams under Nehemiah's direction.

Thirty-eight different leaders are listed, men from at least eight different vocational callings. Seven villages provided volunteers, seven different rulers led community groups, and numerous family relationships are cited—even a man and his daughters. It is clear that all vocations and a full spectrum of age groups are involved. What do these facts reveal? The only way in which the wall could be rebuilt was by people allowing other people to help alongside them.

Already, what at first appears to be a tedious recitation of names begins to throb with life and truth! They needed each other.

People need people. "Not too original," you might say. I agree. But an obvious, oft-repeated truth, frequently disregarded because it lacks flair, is usually "oft repeated" with good reason—it's wise, and it works.

The heart of this text issues a call to open up to other people, yet that is something most of us fear or resist. As it was in ancient Jerusalem, you and I are surrounded by others in whom God is working His plan. He calls both us and those around us to responsibly, honestly, and receptively respond to His purpose in teamwork. In the process of rebuilding, we will find that our progress upward is proportionate to our openness outward: our vertical growth in Christ cannot be dissociated from our horizontal growth with people around us.

I need to remember that I'm not the only person whom God is rebuilding right now. As it was in Nehemiah's day when the whole wall was going up at once, there is today a massive recovery project taking place in and around us. The Holy Spirit is not only restoring the whole you, but He is also seeking to renew the whole church. The implications of that fact are very real at a personal level, for the bottom line of this text's lesson underscores how profoundly we all need each other.

The principal group for you and me that parallels the Jerusalem wall-building team is our spiritual family—our brothers and sisters in Christ. There are people around you who are experiencing the

Holy Spirit's help toward recovering their completeness, maturity, and wholeness in the same way He is helping you. Amid this massive rebuilding effort, we need to learn to relate to one another as members of Christ's body.

Your relationship to and interaction with not only your brothers and sisters in the Lord, but also with all the people who touch your life, is a necessary component of the rebuilding process that the Holy Spirit wants to accomplish in you. The rebuilding of our lives cannot be completed by ourselves. The Holy Spirit is our primary helper, but He has willed to use each of us as instruments in one another's lives.

We need one another in order to help complete who we are to become. This building process doesn't always work easily. How we allow the Holy Spirit to teach us to respond to difficulties we encounter with other people is a rich source of building material toward our wholeness and maturity. People touch our lives in dozens of ways—through domestic, business, community, social, educational, and spiritual relationships, some for years and others just for a moment. Not everyone contributes in the same way. At times, some people may seem to be more of a liability than an asset to your building program. But if we continually remember that we are the Lord's and take the time to ask the Holy Spirit for His point of understanding at each encounter, we will soon find how perfectly and appropriately He has engineered our rebuilding.

Those "Problem People"

Think of somebody you would just rather not spend time with. Find out why. Find out what that person is really like. Take a risk;

you may find that your opinion of the person goes down instead of up if you pursue a relationship. Can you learn to value your differences? The bond of love is dynamic and vital.

Nehemiah lists the people by groups. Each group was working on a specific section of the wall. Some were working near one of the gates. If even one of them had been taken out, hands that were building would be missing, and the others would have had more work. Each one was contributing something. In the same way, all of the people in your life, even the ones you don't particular care for, are contributing something to the rebuilding of your personality.

God wants well-rounded people who can relate to a variety of people, although we can rarely consider ourselves well rounded until our walls have been completed (which means that we have allowed people to work with us). He wants you to stand shoulder to shoulder and reach out to each other. He wants you to risk getting involved with each other. How else will you find out about the pure power that gets released in a group of believers? Don't be deterred by the corruption that has happened in group settings in the past. Risk again.

Notice that people were building "opposite their house." Let people who will build you get involved with you. Your soul needs to be rebuilt on all sides just as Jerusalem's walls needed to be rebuilt on the north, south, east, and west. You *could* decide to eliminate some people from your life, to "de-select" them as friends and colleagues. You would still go to heaven if you did. But you might want to think twice about doing it. Unless that other person is really more of a "Sanballat," chances are that he or she is really serving a helpful purpose in your self-building process. If you eliminate somebody, it might be as if you have decided to feature only one wall of your life, putting all your energy into it. What will happen with those other walls that person was helping you with?

The Word of God reminds us, "For none of us lives to himself, and no one dies to himself" (Rom. 14:7). That one verse summarizes a biblical principle that is far more than a mere social commentary recommending mutual goodwill. It is a conclusive statement from the Holy Spirit teaching us that our lives are irrevocably integrated in the affairs of others. If you try to avoid learning what God wants to do through relationships with people, you withdraw at your own expense and will be poorer for having done so. In short, God is telling us that our growth and healing require us to learn interdependency—in particular with our brothers and sisters in Him—and we will truly gain by doing so.

Coming to a Commitment

Do you find it difficult to relate to people, hesitant to open up or reach out? Issues related to the debris of your past have a way of hindering you from being transparent and vulnerable with others. These problems can become compounded when you allow them to stifle the growth that is possible by your commitment to fellowship with other brothers and sisters in Christ.

Your reluctance to enter relationships or to become too dependent on other people can often be traced to a past association that ended in disappointment and failure. Perhaps you entered into a relationship in trust, only to be left with the debris of brokenness. Your Comforter, the Holy Spirit, has specifically made Himself available to you to heal the wounds of such past relationships, to help you overcome the painful memories, and to avoid being hindered from more of it in the future. He makes it possible for the "new creature" salvation has birthed in us to grow up.

Consider again the different villages, family groups, and leaders who all came together in order to rebuild the wall and the gates. The people of Jerusalem needed to make a commitment to their relationships with one another beyond the rebuilding project itself. This was essential. In the same way, for you and I to sustain a strong life in Jesus Christ once our "walls" have been rebuilt greatly depends on our commitment to relationships with others. Within the body of Christ, we need each other as much beyond the rebuilding project as we do during it.

SUBMITTING TO ONE ANOTHER

The God-given springboard to advancement and growth in healthy, fulfilling relationships is mutual submission.

The Bible says that all believers are to submit "to one another in the fear of God" (Eph. 5:21). "Yes, all of you be submissive to one another, and be clothed with humility" (1 Pet. 5:5). These two direct commands teach that your submission is an evidence of your respect for and reverence for God's purpose, and that we are to do so with a gracious attitude toward the other people in Christ's body.

Notice that the circle of our call to mutual submission remains within the fellowship of faith. The Bible doesn't direct us to submit randomly to just anybody. It calls for this spirit of growth and trust within the community of the redeemed, a growth in relationships and healing among those who have been forgiven and who honestly want to grow forward in Christ's purpose for them.

What does submission mean? Is it a call to become depersonalized or homogenized with the people around me? If I submit, will I need to become somebody's "yes-man"? Will I be placing my welfare at the mercy and whim of others? Is the word *submission* synonymous with self-abnegation—with a "doormat" mentality? Must I learn to let others "walk all over" me? What about individual rights and personal freedom? "Submission" sounds too much like a denial of one's rights.

Let's take a fresh look in the Bible, for if resistance to biblical submission is due to misunderstanding, then understanding holds the key to our responsiveness. We don't want to reject the key to learning about real relationships and thereby miss the key to our growth, all because of misunderstanding one word.

"Submission" is translated from the Greek word *hupotasso* and is derived from the prefixed preposition *hupo* and the verb *tasso*. Technically, it means, "to place under." But in usage, the meaning is not that severe.

First, submission, in its truest sense, can only be *given*; it cannot be exacted. Commanded submission, which entails surrender without the full-hearted consent of the one "submitting," is not truly submissive. Forced submission is actually subjugation—the mastery of one party by another. Submission is voluntary. It implies a choice to trust and a choice to love.

In Greek culture, the fundamental idea of *hupotasso* related to fixed positions of authority and subordination. It was a basic military term describing how to situate people in strategic relationships. It had to do with arranging troops for the purpose of insuring their mutual protection and their collective arrival at victory.

This historical usage can help us understand the word today. I came to understand this meaning of submission through an experience years ago when I was part of a reserve military training program. During my training, I was taught how a small team of soldiers—a squad—was supposed to move forward in enemy territory. Each man had an assigned place in formation following the lead soldier; each was to proceed so as to cover one other soldier. Each soldier needed to perceive his role as vital to the safety and security of the others in his squad, platoon, or company.

Since the military meaning is the essence of the New Testament idea of submission in relationships, it should hold no hint of reducing one another, but only the meaning of protecting each other, of being sensitive to one another, as well as sensible and serving in our relationships with one another. "Submission" includes accountability, and it is not without mutual acknowledgment of appropriate authority. There are no doormats in the kingdom of heaven—only brothers and sisters, sons and daughters of the Father.

The Bible speaks a great deal of this kind of life-to-life relationship with one another: "We, being many, are one body in Christ, and individually members of one another" (Rom. 12:5). Being "joined and knit together by what every joint supplies...causes growth of the body for the edifying of itself in love" (Eph. 4:16). That is *hupotasso*—the kind of submission we are called to in Christ's body.

PARTNERING WITH THE BODY OF CHRIST

This was the original New Testament idea in "joining" a church; it was, and can be today, a knitting together of lives into a supportive, healing fellowship. You and I must consider coming to a point at which we acknowledge that the completion of our growth is going to have to involve other brothers and sisters in Christ. In restoring the human personality, I come to terms with the fact that, just as Jerusalem's wall would never have been completed without each Jew partnering with the rest, so I am only going to be put together through interrelationships with other members of the body of Christ. As Nehemiah led these ancient Jews in a rebuilding partnership, the Holy Spirit wants to lead us in relationships to one another.

He wants us to be surrounded by others, doing our local thing—together. He loves circles of fellowship. Don't withdraw. If you do, you risk developing a breach in the building of part of the wall of your soul.

We need to open up to real mutual dependence upon one another. That is what healthy congregations are about. That's why the holy dynamic of small-group fellowships is so effective, for in such settings the healing love of God flows down to the members of Christ's body.

In that life flow, yet another mighty thing will occur. Jesus said, "When you love one another, the world is going to believe." (See John 17:21.) He assured us in advance what has been proven again and again. As outsiders see the love shown and the mutual blessing realized by Christians who grow together, they say, "I would love to be a part of that kind of thing. These people really care about each other." The net result of wholeness in the body of Christ is evangelism of the lost. Submission is neither an isolated activity of people who surrender personhood nor an exercise in religious piety. It is dynamic, as was the progress on the building of Jerusalem's walls.

Skim Nehemiah 3, and you will see how many repetitions occur: "After him…next to him…After him…next to him…" People were involved *together* in the repairing and rebuilding process, and everyone, every day, could see the fruit of their unity.

Today, those who stand with us in Christ are part of God's program for helping us get the job done. We need them, but they need us too. Our submission to one another makes way for a great building process to be accomplished. If you are not yet in a community of believers, join with a group of brothers and sisters who are committed to growing in Christ as a caring group.

Perhaps you have resisted this need for growth in relationships because of having been hurt by people in the church. Don't avoid the blessing of this commitment because of past hurts. Sadly, some have been wounded in church relationships, or maybe they just didn't like the way they were treated. Perhaps you or someone you know was even sorely misunderstood or cruelly violated. But it wasn't the "relationship" that didn't work; it was people who didn't function in the spirit of Christ!

Moreover, make no mistake: you and I have sometimes been "those people" who hurt others. We must honestly admit that we can all be so blind to our own personal shortcomings that we have probably failed at times to see how we ourselves contributed to some relational disappointments. There have certainly been times when innocent people suffered great wrong at the hands of Christian institutions. But the response to sad history is not isolation.

Someone said years ago, "There are no Lone Rangers in the kingdom of God. Even the Lone Ranger needed Tonto." The need and the scriptural call to healing fellowship are clear.

Fruitfulness and fulfillment can only happen in the context of relationships with people. The way we relate to each other—even when the going gets rough—contributes to the rebuilding process in our own lives. In a dynamic way, we are "edifying" each other, building each other up, even in times of conflict.

Doesn't this sound something like rebuilding the walls of Jerusalem? We have been teamed up with people all around us. In that milieu, we build each other up. Even when it feels like we're doing all of the giving, assisting, and encouraging, we will be transformed and strengthened ourselves in the process.

On my first Sunday at what became The Church On The Way in Van Nuys, California, only a handful of people were in attendance. I welcomed a woman who was obviously a guest, asking her where she normally attended church.

Loftily, she informed me that she did not belong to any particular church, enunciating with "an attitude" that she was simply a member of "the Church" *everywhere*. I didn't communicate my regret for her smallness of understanding. At the same time, she presumed she understood everything she needed to. The church of our Lord Jesus Christ *is* global and larger than any part of it, but the biblical truth is each of us need to be in a local church family. (See 1 Corinthians 16:15–16.)

You can't belong to "the Church" without opening to people. Jesus wants our lives to intersect with His family in a church home where we can grow. No one can thrive and survive by remaining aloof. It's as simple and as basic as that.

So acknowledge your membership. Be part of a church family, and receive the healing and growth that will come to your personality through others. Say, "I am a part of this body," and acknowledge it to the eldership or pastoral leadership in that assembly. Such open declaration is the biblical pattern of submitting to and receiving one another. It's saying, "This place is where I companion with other believers. I'm not just a religious roustabout. I'm a person who, as in Nehemiah, is 'next to…who is next to…who is next to…'" Together, we will be built up together as a "spiritual house in Christ." (See 1 Peter 2:5.)

Chapter 12

THE ADVERSARY

W E HAVE OBSERVED THAT Sanballat, the governor of Samaria and Jerusalem, behaved very much as Satan does in our lives.

As the Holy Spirit is in the process of bringing us into abundant life, we may become weary under the relentless barrage of the adversary's tactics. Even though our destiny is in heaven, we haven't always seen hell vanquished in our personalities.

Satan knows that his authority over you was broken with Christ's entry of the Lord Jesus into your life, but that doesn't stop his assaults. He will try to hinder God's program for you in every way possible. Wherever physical, mental, emotional, or other personal needs remain, he will seek to remove your hope and weaken your confidence. His tactics often work. In many people's lives, he has managed to obstruct progress to the point of halting it. Satan knows he can't get us to hell, but he fires potshots from hell at us, and some of those hit their target.

As the kingdom of God advances in one human life after another, the one who has the "governorship" of the earth gets upset.

Sanballat shows us a picture of Satan's tactics, and Nehemiah's response shows us exactly what we should do to resist them—while we get on with the work of rebuilding.

Earlier, as the building effort began, Sanballat had laughed in open disdain at the Jews, seeking by mockery to discourage them and break their morale. But then the situation intensified: "He was furious and very indignant..." (Neh. 4:1). Sanballat's fury was now at the boiling point. As Nehemiah continued to pull the people together for the rebuilding project, Sanballat saw his hold weakening and his capacity for successful opposition disappearing.

Today, Satan's fury has increased, because these are the latter days spoken of in the Book of Revelation. "The devil has come down to you, having great wrath, because he knows that he has a short time" (Rev. 12:12). Daniel described the efforts of hell in the last days as bent on "wearing out" those who serve God. (See Daniel 7:25, KJV.)

But I am persuaded that irrespective of how bleak the circumstances may seem, or how shadowed the horizons may appear by reason of the adversary's desperate and despicable tactics, Jesus has bequeathed to us a life of power and triumph in the resources of His kingdom. His Holy Spirit is still here to help us realize it. The Lord Jesus has not called us to futility but to victory, and we can learn the path to His dominion over the devil. We can experience full deliverance and joy in believing.

The Enemy's Relentless Attack

Settle your mind on this, loved ones: Satan never has a "good" day. Some people apparently labor under the illusion that the devil may occasionally back off from his attack, as though he might rise on a sunny morning and say, "I think I'll go easy on 'em today." Forget it. It will never be the case. Our adversary, the thief, comes only, as Jesus said, to steal, to kill, and to destroy (John 10:10). That's his entire program. Wrath, great indignation, and mockery constitute the "Sanballat syndrome," and it's the same for the devil.

Nehemiah 4 says that Sanballat rose to speak before his brethren, the army of Samaria. Let's simply consider the "army of Samaria" the same as demons, the army of hell. Satan has a power structure just as Sanballat had an army. We don't wrestle against flesh and blood, but against hosts of demons (principalities and powers) who have rankings in the spirit realm. (See Ephesians 6:12.)

Sanballat made five statements, each of which shows us something. He accused the Jews of:

1. Being feeble
2. Being rebellious
3. Not being able to sacrifice (worship)
4. Not having enough patience or time
5. Lacking resources

First: "What are these feeble Jews doing?" His mocking statement was not directed to the Jews; Sanballat was giving a pep talk to his troops. His first observation relates to the tactical vulnerability of "these feeble Jews." What Sanballat was really doing was lamenting the fact that, until now, he had had complete control. As long as the Jews had no defenses, he could dominate them at will. While he was the governor of the entire region, and until Nehemiah's authority preempted it, his rule was unchallenged. But now, his only point of comfort is that his former subjects were still weakened, though their situation was changing rapidly.

The lesson here is this: don't let the devil remind you of your weakness when his real concern is his loss of power over you! The Spirit of God has come to dwell in you, and the Word of God declares that, "He who is in you is greater than he who is in the world" (1 John 4:4).

Silence the snide attacks of Satan with your own declaration: "I may be weak in myself, but I don't stand alone." You'll discover, as Paul did when he was under satanic attack, "When I am weak, then I am strong." Whatever weakness still remains, Jesus speaks the comforting words, "My grace is sufficient for you. My strength is made perfect in your weakness." (See 2 Corinthians 12:7–10.)

HE ATTACKS YOUR FRAILTIES

Second, Sanballat asked, "Will they fortify themselves?" Later he would raise the question as to Nehemiah's motivation, suggesting that the rebuilding of the walls was a latent conspiracy against Artaxerxes. In truth, Sanballat couldn't care less how the king felt. His concern was the loss of his own control, and he wanted the people with Nehemiah to think he had the king's interests at heart.

Have you ever noticed how amazingly noble Satan can suddenly become when he wants to intimidate a person? He'll say, "Be careful. Don't you see the real reason for trying to rebuild your life? You're just trying to gain independence—you're going to lose your humility. When you get it all together, you're going to stop trusting

God. It's more honorable for you to remain in a defeated, enfeebled condition."

Some of his devices along this line of reasoning include:

- "God somehow wants you sick because you'll trust Him more when you aren't well."
- "It's the will of God that you have financial difficulty. It keeps you humble and dependent."
- "It's the will of God for your business affairs to be under stress; it develops your character."

Of course, a relative truth is present: pressure does cultivate faith and growth in character. But the absolute truth is more significant. Make no mistake—the devil isn't interested in your weakness for godly reasons. He wants to exploit your weakness, unlike God, who wants to bring you to complete strength.

Sanballat's comment "They'll fortify and rebel" is only reflective of Satan's concern with his lost dominion. It also indicates the incredible lengths to which He will go to create doubt that it is God's will for you to be fully restored.

Our souls are full of rubble—unforgiveness, bitterness, bad attitudes, bad habits, painful memories, confusion. Satan will exploit these things. In response to his mocking, declare, "The Holy Spirit is actively helping me to rebuild the ruined walls of the real me!" Even at points where the rubble may be partly your own fault, don't let the adversary get away with his ploy. Take the same stance Nehemiah took with Sanballat!

Your spirit (represented by the rebuilt temple) is protected by the blood of Jesus. Just as the spirit of death could not breach the homes in Egypt that had blood over the doors, your spirit is kept alive by Jesus's blood.

But the rubble all around your spirit can look worse than a highway construction zone. Satan can hook into circumstantial "stuff" that is still lying around the construction site. He can play on old doubts, aggravate unhealed wounds in your soul, and stir up old habits of negative speech. He can chew you up and spit you out—unless you quench his "fiery darts" with the river of life that's flowing from within. Fend the doubts off before they lodge, using your shield of faith, recognizing that your shield of faith grows more effective as your knowledge of the Word grows.

You have two resources: (1) the Word to defend against attack, and (2) the Spirit to quench fiery darts that seem to slip through your first defense. As you partner with the Spirit, the full arsenal of weapons can be deployed.

You can tell the adversary that he has no right to talk like that, "no...right or memorial in Jerusalem" (Neh. 2:20). "For the weapons of our warfare are not carnal but mighty in God for pulling down strongholds" (2 Cor. 10:4).

He Attacks Your Worship of God

Sanballat's next cutting remark before his troops was, "Will they offer sacrifices?" In other words, will they still worship God once they're fortified?

We know the temple was finished and functional, but of course, the walls were still piles of stones. Up to now, the Jews had been defenseless. They were still open prey, even when they went to worship in the temple, and when they went to the temple, they still had to walk past the rubble of the walls. Do you see how this may resemble any clutter in your own life?

As long as the walls of the city were still in rubble, the liberty of the people to come and go freely to worship remained under threat, for their city was unprotected. Further, their critics could still mock, "Look at this rubble. Some God! Some city!" Satan loves to capitalize on our weakness and shame.

This is the satanic spirit evident in Sanballat's question, "Will they offer sacrifices?" Has Satan ever said such things to you: "Who do you think you are? How can you be a believer? What nerve to openly, declaratively, and publicly worship your God when your life still shows signs of the past. God isn't going to listen to you. You'll never qualify as a real worshiper!"

But the answer to this mocking question is, "Yes! I will worship!" I will worship without impediment, because God has taken hold in my heart and I know my true identity. I am at peace. My mind is stayed on the Lord, not on my history or on my rubble.

HE MOCKS THE SLOWNESS OF YOUR PROGRESS

In his fourth challenge, Sanballat insinuated that they would never get the task done: "Will they complete it in a day?" It's the same kind of mockery the adversary whispers to us: "Talk all you want, but you've attempted this before; you may have spent a long time thinking about it, but it didn't work then, and it won't happen now either."

From the text, we are given no idea how long this wall-rebuilding project might have been on the drawing board—probably long before Nehemiah's visit. We do know the temple had been completed about seventy years earlier, and there is every reason to believe that plans for rebuilding the wall had existed for a long time. Now it was underway, but it didn't look like much yet.

Progress was slow, and the people were already tired. (See Nehemiah 4:10.) So what does Sanballat imply here? Their adversary seeks to insert a soul-wearying loss of tenacity into their faith.

It's the same with you and me. When things seem to drag on and on, he'll chortle at you, "In a day? Hah!" But lay hold of the whole story. Your "Nehemiah"—the Holy Spirit—has come. Listen to Him when you don't see quick progress, and when the enemy plays on that problem, the Comforter has the answer: "Do not grow weary while doing good, for in due season you shall reap if you do not lose heart." (See Galatians 6:9.)

God's promise is certain. The completion may not be today, but the promise is His guarantee. Discouragement may work for a while, but let's be frank in our reply: "No, of course the rebuilding won't happen in one day. But there are treasures buried in my soul's rubble, and my God is here to help me."

HE RIDICULES YOUR BUILDING MATERIALS

Finally, Sanballat spouted, "Will they revive the stones from the heaps of rubbish—stones that are burned?" (Neh. 4:2).

As you will recall, when Nehemiah arrived, the only material he brought for the rebuilding program was timber. Thus, logically you might ask, "Where will they get the materials for the walls?" The answer is thrilling in its significance to our lives: the walls will be completed by reclaiming, retooling, restoring, and recovering the very stones that comprise the current mess!

What a message of hope that picture contains, and its truth applies to you. God is able to so completely redeem and restore, He can glorify Himself in the midst of, and out of, the rubble of our broken past! He is willing to remove the humiliation and pain of the past and to put those broken pieces back together. Jesus Himself declared the fulfillment of Isaiah's prophecy: "The Spirit of the LORD is upon Me...to heal the brokenhearted" (Luke 4:18). The same Holy Spirit is prepared to rebuild your new life and raise it up in splendor. It's true! How often have you heard people testify of the Lord taking the rubble of their failure and building something worthwhile?

It's often past failures that the Lord will use to rebuild the walls. In the meantime, the peace of God will guard you. (See Philippians 4:6–7.) The Holy Spirit will do sentry duty. Don't weary your soul over uncertainties represented by the rubble of the past.

Here's an example of how this works: Awhile ago, I made a commitment that I subsequently found I could not keep. I was not only embarrassed when I found myself unable to fulfill it, but I was further shamed to realize that the commitment had been made presumptuously, not out of godly dependence on the Spirit. The situation was more than awkward. I felt I was a discredit to the Lord and to my pastoral office.

I sought God in prayer repentantly. As I did, I felt directed to simply write a forthright letter to all of the parties involved in the situation—which involved about five hundred men! Without self-defense, I acknowledged my misjudgment, told them that I couldn't keep my commitment, and asked for their forgiveness. I also confessed my conviction that I had acted vainly and stupidly, and I humbly described my now-recognizable pride. An amazing thing happened.

Not only did God forgive me, and the men too, but also the whole situation turned around. Out of an occasion that might have been blighted by my failure, God made a building block. Before it was over, the triumph that occurred exceeded everyone's brightest expectations. Only God can do that.

Let your own hope rise, even in the face of any actual wastefulness or foolishness related to your past. Be assured; in spite of what has happened to you, God is able to recover, reclaim, restore, renew, and rebuild whatever has been broken. He will bring full restoration to your life, your personality, your character, your mind, to whatever part of you has been crushed, bruised, broken, stained, tarnished, or ruined—even if a good part of it is due to your own miscalculations.

Bring your brokenness out into the light, no matter what Satan's Sanballat-like accusations may be. Learn to recognize the adversary's tactics.

LOTR: Eowyn vs. Worm -word The city .... not Gondor... the Eowyn City.

That's all he is—an adversary to an ongoing work of God. He can try to interfere, but he doesn't have the final word. As the "governor" of your soul, he never made any effort to help you rebuild. Now Someone who is more powerful has superseded his authority, and he's not happy about it.

Aren't you glad you have your Nehemiah?

Chapter 13

STRATEGIES ON THE WALL

OTICE THE PROGRESSION OF the degree of threat as the wall-rebuilding progresses. Sanballat and his men came back ten times, first coming with only mockery (Neh. 4:1–2), then with a general threat ("we will come against you," verse 8), and finally with an forceful announcement ("we will come in," verse 11).

When they saw that the walls had been rebuilt to half their height, Sanballat and his allies became more organized in their opposition against the builders. Their plan was threefold: intimidate, demoralize, and defeat. They badgered, mocked, and threatened the workers with everything, including beatings and death, should they stick with the rebuilding project. (See Nehemiah 4:11.)

That their efforts failed is a testimony to Nehemiah's counter-strategies and also to the hard-pressed wall builders' persistence.

As is always the case with Satan, there is a complete absence of any justification for Sanballat's hatefulness; only good was taking place at Jerusalem. But Nehemiah took this threat seriously, and the Scriptures record his strategy for defense: (1) he inspires faith, (2) he equips and positions against attack, and (3) he presses the work forward.

Nehemiah called to the people, "Don't be afraid! Remember the Lord!" (Neh. 4:14, TLB). Then he placed the people in position "according to their families" (v. 13), a tactic that combines sound military strategy with morale-building relationships. This sounds like the way the Holy Spirit draws us together and teaches us to strengthen each other with mutual encouragement. Not only does this unity comfort and strengthen us, but also satanic plots are defused "where two or three are gathered together" in Jesus's name (Matt. 18:20).

> So it was, from that time on, that half of my servants worked at construction, while the other half held the spears, the shields, the bows, and wore armor.... Every one of the builders had his sword girded at this side as he built.
>
> —Nehemiah 4:16, 18

Just as Nehemiah did not discount the capacity of Sanballat to succeed in destroying the work and the workers, the New Testament perspective on the enemy of our souls advises serious-mindedness: "Be sober, be vigilant; because your adversary the devil walks about like a roaring lion, seeking whom he may devour" (1 Pet. 5:8). There is no reason for us to fear defeat, but neither is there reason for us to doubt there will be battle.

Escalating Threats

The Jews who lived outside the city and who therefore dwelt closer to the adversaries reported these threats: "They tell us that every day when we're finished with our day's work and we come back through the still-broken segments of the wall to go home for the night, they're going to break in on us through those still-broken places. No longer will we be free to come and go." (See Nehemiah 4:12.) For their safety and for the progress of the work, Nehemiah assigned some of the builders to live in the city.

It's the same with us as we learn to "live in the new us" the Holy Spirit is rebuilding. Jesus tells us, "In your patience possess ye your souls" (Luke 21:19, KJV). The people were going back home over the remaining broken places every night. For the present, they weren't using the gates since they were not yet erected. It's wise to learn from their experience to avoid walking in and out of our days, constantly reviewing our remaining weaknesses. Instead, review the victories, praise God for what has been rebuilt, and learn to live in your "rebuilt self."

HIGH PLACES, LOW PLACES

Because of this threat, people were set in position to guard. (See Nehemiah 4:13.) Nehemiah is such a picture of the Holy Spirit—he takes his position *in the parts of the wall where the most is yet to be accomplished.*

We learn here how the adversary will approach those points in the soul where there has not yet been full restoration. Welcome the Holy Spirit to defend you in those lower places, which are still half rubble, while accepting responsibility to stand firm where the walls have been completed. Just as Nehemiah directed them to position a defense on the higher parts of the rebuilt wall, take your position. Similarly, the Holy Spirit calls us to responsibility to keep guard on that which has been restored. Paul said, "Stand fast in the liberty by which Christ has made us free, and do not be entangled again in the yoke of bondage." (See Galatians 5:1.) We are called to hold our position firmly. Don't yield to the past. Invite His power, but it's your choice to take your position.

You say, "My problem is the broken places, where it's not finished yet." Well, the Holy Spirit says, like Nehemiah, "I will set Myself in the lower places." Praise God. The Holy Spirit will take up guard at the entry points, and He will defend you. Lord, thank You for Your superintending ministry.

The Holy Spirit Himself will be defending you in your current broken places. Where are you being tempted? Where are you afraid that the enemy is going to break in? That's where He'll be, defending you.

Working and Guarding

Just as Nehemiah made the people look to him, saying, "Be not afraid," we need to listen to the Holy Spirit when He whispers the same thing. He will flow strength and courage into us. God is our strong defender; He's not merely uttering empty reassurances. Never! He speaks as a formidable foe to any power that threatens us, His beloved sons and daughters. He can overthrow every effort of the adversary as He rises in us!

> And it happened, when our enemies heard that it was known to us, and that God had brought their plot to nothing, that all of us returned to the wall, everyone to his work. So it was, from that time on, that half of my servants worked at construction, while the other half held

the spears, the shields, the bows, and wore armor; and the leaders were behind all the house of Judah. Those who built on the wall, and those who carried burdens, loaded themselves so that with one hand they worked at construction, and with the other held a weapon. Every one of the builders had his sword girded at his side as he built. And the one who sounded the trumpet was beside me.

Then I said to the nobles, the rulers, and the rest of the people, "The work is great and extensive, and we are separated far from one another on the wall. Wherever you hear the sound of the trumpet, rally to us there. Our God will fight for us."

So we labored in the work, and half of the men held the spears from daybreak until the stars appeared.

—NEHEMIAH 4:15–21

As the people listened to the counsel of Nehemiah (the Holy Spirit), the counsel of the enemy were brought to naught and the enemies knew it. The Word of God is the counsel that the Lord gives to you.

Note that it was half of Nehemiah's servants who worked while half guarded. This doesn't refer to the people at large, who were not Nehemiah's servants. It refers to the contingent who had come with Nehemiah at the beginning, his "captains of the army and horsemen" (Neh. 2:9).

In our personal rebuilding projects, this shows us how the Spirit sets a guard over us. He doesn't expect it to be accomplished by the laborers themselves, but rather He sets guards from His own forces—the angels. Angels are ministering spirits sent to minister on behalf of us. (See Hebrews 1:13–14.)

> He shall give His angels charge over you,
> To keep you in all your ways.
> In their hands they shall bear you up,
> Lest you dash your foot against a stone.
>
> —Psalm 91:11–12

Angels are involved in the work! The Holy Spirit is the commander in chief of the angelic hosts. He sends them to help us individually.

So the Holy Spirit defends us in the weak places, and we resist the devil in the high places. Wherever we remain weak and easily breached, an angelic guard supplies protection. But wherever our walls have been refortified, "we the people" can supply both protection and more rebuilding—because we have *swords*. Like the Jews of that era, we too have swords—the sword of the Word.

We've all had the experience of God invisibly sustaining us by angelic aid, but we're called to also learn to wield the sword of His Word as we join in resisting the adversary.

The Sound of the Trumpet

Nehemiah speaks to the rulers about the sound of the trumpet, which would unite them in their scatteredness along the length of the wall (Neh. 4:19–20).

We too hear a trumpet call: "Forsake not the assembling of yourselves together." (See Hebrews 10:25.) The message is very clear: we need the Word, and we need the growth and strength of fellowship at our church home.

Healing comes from the body. It's as if you have a cut on your finger. You need healing. You don't need to amputate it and set it aside. If it stays attached to your body, it can be healed. Don't let your bad feelings keep you from assembling, because that's when you need the body the most.

The people started staying within the city at night, where they were safer. Before, they had gone back to where they lived among the other Jews, and they had heard the threats daily. They were beaten down in spirit, uncertain about when the "other shoe would drop." Nehemiah said, "You need to live in here now."

The Lord doesn't call us to isolation from the world but to *insulation* from it. He calls us to dwell in Zion. (See Isaiah 30:19.)

STANDING STRONG

Satan is at work, but that is not the whole story, for the final truth is this: You can stand! You can win! And you can launch a triumphant counterattack!

Nehemiah's direction and equipping of the Jerusalemites for resistance and victory display timeless principles:

1. The adversary is real, and his threats are real threats.

2. The battle is crucial; defeat or victory is at stake.

3. Victory is certain when God's people draw on His resources.

There is no escaping the reality of spiritual warfare, and there is no running from its implications. Paul spoke of the adversary's tactics, saying, "We are not ignorant of his devices" (2 Cor. 2:11), noting that where such ignorance prevails, Satan gains a distinct advantage.

The Holy Spirit is your ever-present Comforter—here today to show the way to secure the "city" of your own soul and personal circumstances and to bring victory against every satanic onslaught.

Part Four

STRONG AND SECURE

And there was a great outcry of the people and their wives against their Jewish brethren....

And I became very angry when I heard their outcry....After serious thought, I rebuked the nobles and rulers, and said to them, "Each of you is exacting usury from his brother." So I called a great assembly against them....Then I said, "What you are doing is not good....Please, let us stop this usury! Restore now to them, even this day, their lands, their vineyards, their olive groves, and their houses, also a hundredth of the money and the grain, the new wine and the oil, that you have charged them."

So they said, "We will restore *it,* and will require nothing from them; we will do as you say."

Then I called the priests, and required an oath from them that they would do according to this promise. Then I shook out the fold of my garment and said, "So may God shake out each man from his house, and from his property, who does not perform this promise. Even thus may he be shaken out and emptied." And all the assembly said, "Amen!" and praised the Lord. Then the people did according to this promise....

Now it happened when Sanballat, Tobiah, Geshem the Arab, and the rest of our enemies heard that I had rebuilt the wall, and that there were no breaks left in it (though at that time I had not hung the doors in the gates), that Sanballat and Geshem sent to me, saying, "Come, let us meet together among the villages in the plain of Ono." But they thought to do me harm.

So I sent messengers to them, saying, "I am doing a great work, so that I cannot come down. Why should the work cease while I leave it and go down to you?"

But they sent me this message four times, and I answered them in the same manner....For they all were trying to make us afraid, saying, "Their hands will be weakened in the work, and it will not be done."

Now therefore, O God, strengthen my hands....

So the wall was finished on the twenty-fifth day of Elul, in fifty-two days....

Then it was, when the wall was built and I had hung the doors, when the gatekeepers, the singers, and the Levites had been appointed, that I gave the charge of Jerusalem to my brother Hanani, and Hananiah the leader of the citadel, for he was a faithful man and feared God more than many. And I said to them, "Do not let the gates of Jerusalem be opened until the sun is hot; and while they stand guard, let them shut and bar the doors; and appoint guards from among the inhabitants of Jerusalem, one at his watch station and another in front of his own house."...

Now all the people gathered together as one man in the open square that was in front of the Water Gate; and they told Ezra the scribe to bring the Book of the Law of Moses, which the Lord had commanded Israel. So Ezra the priest brought the Law before the assembly, of men and women and all who could hear with understanding on the first day of the seventh month. Then he read from it in the open square that was in front of the Water Gate from morning until midday, before the men and women and those who could understand; and the ears of all the people were attentive to the Book of the Law.

So Ezra the scribe stood on a platform of wood which they had made for the purpose.... And Ezra opened the book in the sight of all the people, for he was standing above all the people; and when he opened it, all the people stood up. And Ezra blessed the LORD, the great God. Then all the people answered, "Amen, Amen!" while lifting up their hands. And they bowed their heads and worshiped the LORD with their faces to the ground...and the Levites, helped the people to understand the Law; and the people stood in their place. So they read distinctly from the book, in the Law of God; and they gave the sense, and helped them to understand the reading.

And Nehemiah, who was the governor, Ezra the priest and scribe, and the Levites who taught the people said to all the people, "This day is holy to the LORD your God; do not mourn nor weep." For all the people wept, when they heard the words of the Law. Then he said to them, "Go your way, eat the fat, drink the sweet, and send portions to those for whom nothing is prepared; for this day is holy to our LORD. Do not sorrow, for the joy of the LORD is your strength."...

...Now at the dedication of the wall of Jerusalem they sought out the Levites in all their places, to bring them to Jerusalem to celebrate the dedication with gladness, both with thanksgivings and singing, with cymbals and stringed instruments and harps.... So I brought the leaders of Judah up on the wall, and appointed two large thanksgiving choirs....

...the two thanksgiving choirs stood in the house of God, likewise I and the half of the rulers with me.... The singers sang loudly with Jezrahiah the director. Also that day they offered great sacrifices, and rejoiced, for God had made them rejoice with great joy; the women and the children also rejoiced, so that the joy of Jerusalem was heard afar off....

...Now before this, Eliashib the priest, having authority over the storerooms of the house of our God, was allied with Tobiah. And he had prepared for him a large room, where previously they had stored the grain offerings, the frankincense, the articles, the tithes of grain, the new wine and oil, which were commanded to be given to the Levites and singers and gatekeepers, and the offerings for the priests. But during all this I was not in Jerusalem, for in the thirty-second year of Artaxerxes king of Babylon I had returned to the king. Then after certain days I obtained leave from the king, and I came to Jerusalem and discovered the evil that Eliashib had done for Tobiah, in preparing a room for him in the courts of the house of God. And it grieved me bitterly; therefore I threw all the household goods of Tobiah out of the room. Then I commanded them to cleanse the rooms;

and I brought back into them the articles of the house of God, with the grain offering and the frankincense.

I also realized that the portions for the Levites had not been given them; for each of the Levites and the singers who did the work had gone back to his field. So I contended with the rulers, and said, "Why is the house of God forsaken?" And I gathered them together and set them in their place....

In those days I saw people in Judah treading wine presses on the Sabbath, and bringing in sheaves, and loading donkeys with wine, grapes, figs, and all kinds of burdens, which they brought into Jerusalem on the Sabbath day. And I warned them about the day on which they were selling provisions. Men of Tyre dwelt there also, who brought in fish and all kinds of goods, and sold them on the Sabbath to the children of Judah, and in Jerusalem. Then I contended with the nobles of Judah, and said to them, "What evil thing is this that you do, by which you profane the Sabbath day? Did not your fathers do thus, and did not our God bring all this disaster on us and on this city? Yet you bring added wrath on Israel by profaning the Sabbath."

So it was, at the gates of Jerusalem, as it began to be dark before the Sabbath, that I commanded the gates to be shut, and charged that they must not be opened till after the Sabbath. Then I posted some of my servants at the gates, so that no burdens would be brought in on the Sabbath day. Now the merchants and sellers of all kinds of wares lodged outside Jerusalem once or twice. So I warned them, and said to them, "Why do you spend the night around the wall? If you do so again, I will lay hands on you!" From that time on they came no more on the Sabbath. And I commanded the Levites that they should cleanse themselves, and that they should go and guard the gates, to sanctify the Sabbath day.

Remember me, O my God, concerning this also, and spare me according to the greatness of Your mercy!

In those days I also saw Jews who had married women of Ashdod, Ammon, and Moab. And half of their children spoke the language of Ashdod, and could not speak the language of Judah, but spoke according to the language of one or the other people. So I contended with them and cursed them, struck some of them and pulled out their hair, and made them swear by God, saying, "You shall not give your daughters as wives to their sons, nor take their daughters for your sons or yourselves. Did not Solomon king of Israel sin by these things? Yet among many nations there was no king like him, who was beloved of his God; and God made him king over all Israel. Nevertheless pagan women caused even him to sin. Should we then hear of your doing all this great evil, transgressing against our God by marrying pagan women?"…

Thus I cleansed them of everything pagan. I also assigned duties to the priests and the Levites, each to his service, and to bringing the wood offering and the firstfruits at appointed times.

Remember me, O my God, for good!

—Nehemiah 5:1–13; 6:1–15; 7:1–3; 8:1–10;
12:27–43; 13:4–31

Chapter 14

BUILT UP TO GROW UP

===

I HAVE OFTEN FOUND IT more difficult for people to accept responsibility for their part in the process of redemptive restoration they are willing to welcome God's divine grace. Yet the success of our restoration calls for a balance of both—to accept His grace but also to answer His call to grow up. So, let's now deal with learning to live life in the "rebuilt city."

DEPENDENT RESPONSIBILITY

Understanding God's call to responsibility involves the challenge of walking a delicate balance. God's insistence on us accepting our own responsibility is not a resignation on His part from His ongoing willingness to love, provide, sustain, and empower us. Our acceptance of fuller assignments and duty as we are renewed and are growing in Christ does not presume that we have outgrown our place of dependence on Him.

The story in Jerusalem presents a practical case of this balance between dependence and responsibility. The rebuilding program was moving toward completion. Things were looking great! Huge segments of the wall now stood silhouetted against the sky as testimonies to God's faithfulness, Nehemiah's leadership, and the people's responsible participation. All that remained to be done was to finish some stonework on the walls, to be followed shortly by the building and hanging of the great gates.

Sanballat and Tobiah had not been silenced, but they had been rendered ineffective; their threats, mockings, and conspiratorial designs had all been resisted and overthrown.

But suddenly, "there was a great outcry of the people and their wives against their…brethren" (Neh. 5:1). The people themselves were on the verge of defeating the project from within, after outside enemies had been so successfully resisted. After having been protected and delivered from the oppression of Sanballat and his cronies, they were now oppressing each other.

NEHEMIAH GETS ANGRY

Jerusalem was in disarray. Nehemiah chapter 5 shows the people in debt, being eaten up by taxes, their children being put into slavery to pay debts, and families at one another's throats. How could this be? This is Jew against fellow Jew. Nehemiah got *mad*!

I love Nehemiah's capacity for anger. Since he prefigures the Holy Spirit, some people might presume that he would be incapable of indignation, especially violent indignation. But this capacity is not inconsistent with the Holy Spirit, for He is not only characterized by the gentleness of a dove but also as the Spirit of judgment and burning: "For our God is a consuming fire" (Heb. 12:29). The Holy Spirit is quite able to respond angrily to being resisted, grieved, and sinned against: "But they rebelled and grieved His Holy Spirit;

so He turned Himself against them as an enemy, and He fought against them" (Isa. 63:10).

It is important to keep His anger in context. Remember, God's anger and resulting actions always seek the ultimate good of the people involved. His vengeance is never vindictive, but confrontational and bold to judge against evil. He won't stand for it, nor will He allow us to willfully, ignorantly push forward unto error. Since He cares enough to restore us, He cares enough to confront us. His loving tenderness does not preempt a potent readiness to discipline.

Nehemiah was serious about the subject of responsibility. He required the people to maintain their lives and their city under divine government. The goal of God's restoration programs will always be to beget responsible self-government instead of slothful self-indulgence. The Holy Spirit wants the Jerusalem of your life to be a city of the great King—one where His kingdom life is lived and served.

The people were oppressing each other in ways that sound familiar to us because we ourselves have been oppressors—or the oppressed—in some of the same ways:

1. They were financially overextended and victims of economic frustration. Their concern that their children be fed was commendable, but it was manifesting itself in strife, discord, and interpersonal conflict. (See Nehemiah 5:1–2.)

2. Hungry and under great pressure, they had made financial decisions that seemed necessary but that

were only creating deeper problems. By mortgaging their property or deferring tax payments to ease financial pressure, they were only using stopgap solutions, and now these mistakes were coming back to haunt them. (See Nehemiah 5:3–4.)

3. Amid the pressures of life, their children (who were earlier the source of their solicitous concern) had become slaves, sold by their own parents under pressure in order to meet their debtors' demands. (See Nehemiah 5:5.)

Who needs enemies when you have friends and family like this? Through their strife and mutual exploitation, they had reduced each other to poverty and misery. The same thing can happen to us in mental and emotional ways, even when money is not involved. By unforgiveness, lack of sensitivity, ungraciousness, loveless criticism, judgmentalism, unreceptiveness, bitterness, and the like, we lay burdens on our own shoulders and, as it were, we "tax" others. We even use the phrase, "It was a taxing burden to bear."

How brothers and sisters relate to each other is the ultimate release point that allows the church to really function as a church. These patterns of behavior are the antitheses of wholeness and life in the spirit of Christ Jesus, which entails self-sacrifice:

Then Jesus said to His disciples, "If anyone desires to come after Me, let him deny himself, and take up his cross, and follow Me. For whoever desires to save his life will lose it, but whoever loses his life for My sake will find it. For what profit is it to a man if he gains the whole world, and loses his own soul? Or what will a man give in exchange for his soul? For the Son of Man will come in the glory of His Father with His angels, and then He will reward each according to his works.

—MATTHEW 16:24–27

Jesus, like Nehemiah, makes God's standards clear. It's not as if the people didn't know this already, but they allowed their desire to escape from the pressures of their life to become more important than holiness.

The people of Nehemiah's day, those of Jesus's day, and all of us today fall prey to the same human condition, resorting to pride and domineering behavior. (See Jesus's correction in Matthew 18:3–4.) The people had willfully misled each other and had drawn each other into webs of sin. (See Matthew 18:6–7.) They had tolerated deception and abuses and had excused themselves from having generous and forgiving hearts. (See Matthew 18:15, 21, 35.) They had become judgmental of their own brethren, just as we do, excusing it because, after all, "I have a good reason."

GETTING READY FOR GATES

The gates could not be hung in the wall until this issue of exploitation was dealt with. It's almost as if (given the inevitable condition of the human heart) that the events of chapter 5 of Nehemiah had to occur before the gates could be fixed in position.

In the same way, our personal walls are not complete until we have dealt with forgiveness issues. Then and only then can we be trusted to control our "access and egress" through our gates.

We are allowed to exercise our judgment in order to be discerning about error, and we are supposed to be decisive in terms of worldliness, but we are never given the latitude to be picayunish, loveless, or condescending, including toward the lost, whose lives may well be horribly rebellious and hostile to God.

Responding to the Spirit of God is essential. We will have rebuilt our souls in vain if we refuse to hear His correction. God disciplines those He loves, His chosen sons and daughters. (See Proverbs 3:12; Hebrews 12:6.)

Nehemiah forced the settlement of the issue. He would not let them get this far only to squander the victory. He would not let them end badly.

He is like the Holy Spirit, the "author and finisher of our faith" (Heb. 12:2) who is active in our lives. A "finisher" keeps at it until the whole job is finished. He won't settle for a half-built wall or for gaping holes where the gates should be.

God is not a halfway God. When He begins a work in your life, He *will* bring it to a successful conclusion.

God's desire is to make each of us whole to the degree that we are able to function in the independence wholeness allows. This means we will be able to move forward on our own while remaining wise enough (like children!) to know we need Him— and one another.

There is a sweeping difference between our dependency upon Him during the winter of our recovery from destruction and our reliance on His life and power in the summer of our growth into fruitfulness. As we come to that joyous season, He will require more of us than before, not because we have become self-sufficient, but because He, our Creator, has now restored us to the capacity for responsible self-rule under His overarching government in our souls.

Chapter 15

GLORY IN THE GATES

T HE REBUILT WALLS PROVIDED protection for the city, just as our rebuilt personalities protect us from enemies. But protection can never be complete unless the gates—ten of them, in the case of the city of Jerusalem—are also replaced with new ones.

When Nehemiah had made his first inspection of the ruined city walls, what was left of the gates was still devastated and charred black because of the flames that had burned them generations earlier. He found it just as Hanani had reported: "The wall of Jerusalem is also broken down, and its gates are burned with fire" (Neh. 1:3).

At least four times in Nehemiah 1 and 2, Nehemiah spoke of the gates this way, including them in his statement about the state of destruction of the walls. This makes it plain that the gates were just as important as the walls. Of course it was important to rebuild the walls, but it was equally important to raise up the ten gates into their former glory as part of the fortifications. In fact, the gates have significance that goes beyond that of wall-like protection.

Gates are obviously places of access to and egress from a walled city. But in the ancient world, they were also places of city business. "In the gate" is where a man would go to make announcements, seal contractual agreements, and confirm durable decisions. We find evidence of this fact in the Book of Ruth and in other biblical accounts, as well as by means of archeological discoveries. Civil and legal codes were drawn up and executed in the gates. In short, city government occurred there. The gates of a city were like city hall. Gates were authority centers.

"Gates" are mentioned throughout the Book of Psalms:

> Lift up your heads, O you gates! And be lifted up, you everlasting doors! And the King of glory shall come in.
>
> —Psalm 24:7 (also verse 9)

> The Lord loves the gates of Zion more than all the dwellings of Jacob.
>
> —Psalm 87:2

> Enter into His gates with thanksgiving, and into His courts with praise. Be thankful to Him, and bless His name.
>
> —Psalm 100:4

Even in the Book of Genesis, gates symbolize authority. When Adam and Eve were driven from the Garden of Eden, God set cherubim to guard the gates so that they could not return, barring the way back to the tree of life. (See Genesis 3:24.) We see the special importance of gates right up through the Book of Revelation, where we read about the twelve gates of pearl, through which only the righteous (who are righteous through Christ's blood) have the authority to enter. (See Revelation 21:21.)

So clearly are the city gates significant; they are much more important than ordinary doors. They carried a meaning that went far beyond their function of being open or closed. Gates meant a right of operation for a city. Rehanging the gates was a crowning achievement of the long rebuilding task.

THE TEN GATES

In the almost-completed Jerusalem wall, the ten gates are mentioned by name. They are the Sheep Gate, the Fish Gate, the Old Gate, the Valley Gate, the Dung Gate, the Fountain Gate, the Water Gate, the Horse Gate, the East Gate, and the Miphkad Gate (a name not usually translated and that carries the idea of accounting and responsibility). (See Nehemiah 3:1, 3, 6, 13–15, 26, 28–29, 31–32.) Each of these gates was named because it had become significant to some particular type of business. This includes even the "business" of disposing of waste (through the Dung Gate, also known as the Refuse Gate, which gave access to the burning dump site of the Valley of Hinnom). The Sheep Gate, for instance, was the gate through which the sacrificial sheep were brought to the temple.

Each of the ten gates carried a particular significance, just as each of the keys on your key ring will open or shut a particular door. When you pull your keys out of your pocket, you can exercise your right of access to your car, your office, your house, or to whatever locked door you have a key to. Your keys are a symbol of your authority. Without them, you have to ask permission every time.

So when Jesus said He would give us the keys to the kingdom of heaven in Matthew 16:19, He meant that with His "power keys," you can open and shut, loose and bind within your day-to-day experience. You can govern your life with the authority you have because of Him.

Bible scholars often attribute significance to certain numbers as they are used in Scripture. It is not uncommon to note how the number ten may be seen to represent "human government," just as the number twelve may represent "divine government."

In that light, note how the ten gates of Jerusalem offer a practical parallel to our personal lives.

Just as Nehemiah was committed to restoring the walls and its gates, so the Holy Spirit wants to assist us. He comes to rebuild the walls of defense against the enemy but also seeks to replace the gates. Just as gates controlled the entry and exit of all that would come in or go out of Jerusalem, the Holy Spirit's recovery of self-control in our lives is depicted. He has come to enable a new dimension of dominion to be exercised in our hearts, minds, and emotions—determining actions that reflect our self-control by reason of His renewed "gates" in our lives.

Not Quite So Fast

Step into that ancient scene again because it's the same thing the Comforter—our Nehemiah—wants to repeat today.

Everybody was ready. Each gate had its own team of workers who had constructed the heavy wooden doors out of solid beams and thick planks. Each had been measured to fit the openings perfectly, and the doorframes had been prepared. Pulleys and stout ropes and counterweights were ready at the gate sites. Even with so much prepared ahead of time, it would take a few weeks to complete the hanging of all ten of the gates.

With such excellent organization, not to mention the added burst of energy that often comes near the end of a long and difficult building project, you would think that this would be the easy part, wouldn't you? But that assumption overlooks the newly aggravated malice of the adversary, the same adversary who had opposed every step of the long rebuilding process.

Yes, Sanballat returns.

> Now it happened when Sanballat, Tobiah, Geshem the Arab, and the rest of our enemies heard that I had rebuilt the wall, and that there were no breaks left in it (though at that time I had not hung the doors in the gates), that Sanballat and Geshem sent to me, saying, "Come, let us meet together among the villages in the plain of Ono." But they thought to do me harm. So I sent messengers to them, saying, "I am doing a great work, so that I cannot come down. Why should the work cease while I leave it and go down to you?" But they sent me this message four times, and I answered them in the same manner.
>
> —NEHEMIAH 6:1–4

Do you see how Nehemiah responded to Sanballat's seemingly reasonable request? He showed no respect to the intruder, recognizing his remarks—like Satan's—never have our interests at heart. Remember that when Satan approaches with any of his ploys. He may sound reasonable when he invites you to negotiate with him, but don't be deceived. The Holy Spirit is assisting, and Satan never wants you to uncover the true self-control that is necessary to govern your life.

You can always use Nehemiah's strategy against the enemy. It's easy to do. You won't have to memorize a lengthy passage of Scripture or remember a complicated step one, step two, step three procedure. Your resistance can be expressed in one little word— "No!" You don't even have to say "No, *thanks.*" It's essential to be firm, even rude, when you withstand the enemy. Never wilt before him, but rise in the name of Jesus, even if Satan comes back several times as Sanballat did with Nehemiah. Employ the surefire strategy of the Word of God: "Resist the devil and he will flee from you" (James 4:7).

The gates of self-control are ready to be raised. That's the task to concentrate on now. Don't debate with old enemies; don't negotiate with options the flesh or the devil suggest, even if they repeatedly return with false accusations about your motives in the way Sanballat did to Nehemiah.

> Then Sanballat sent his servant to me as before, the fifth time, with an open letter in his hand. In it was written: It is reported among the nations, and Geshem says, that you and the Jews plan to rebel; therefore, according to these rumors, you are rebuilding the wall, that you may be their king. And you have also appointed prophets to proclaim concerning you at Jerusalem, saying, "There is a king in Judah!" Now these matters will be reported to the king. So come, therefore, and let us consult together.
>
> Then I sent to him, saying, "No such things as you say are being done, but you invent them in your own heart." For

they all were trying to make us afraid, saying, "Their hands
will be weakened in the work, and it will not be done."

Now therefore, O God, strengthen my hands.

—Nehemiah 6:6–9

Sanballat, worried about his own position as governor of Judah,
was sounding a false alarm here, and Nehemiah didn't have any
trouble discerning it. He forcefully answered with the plain truth:
"Nothing you say is true. You're making it all up!" And he immediately went back to his work.

Notice also that Nehemiah prays: "Now therefore, O God,
strengthen my hands." Nehemiah prays often. He doesn't bother to
pray that God will eliminate his enemies. He does pray, however,
that God will strengthen his hands for the work once again, so that
his enemies will be disappointed in their mission to discourage him
and to "weaken his hands."

Your "Gates"

How often have you had the experience of feeling as if you were
shaken and threatened in your own security? Does it seem at times
as if the protective walls of your personality have been breached?
You have been a Christian for years, perhaps decades, and yet some
enemy activity makes you realize that you have gaps in the walls.

The Lord wants to strengthen your will—not in the sense of
your becoming stubborn or rebellious but in the righteous sense
of your gaining sturdiness of character and purpose, integrity and
wholeness. He wants you to be secure in Him, "secured" within the
stronghold of His salvation, impregnable to the enemy, no matter
what mode of attack he launches.

He wants you to let Him restore government in your own life. It may take a long time. We're all at different places, and each of us has more than one "gate." Not all of your gates will be hung and secured at the same moment.

This part of the Book of Nehemiah portrays quite a different scene from the first chapters of the book. Earlier chapters are concerned with the wall-rebuilding process, including the necessary defense against adversaries. Now that the wall-building itself is pretty much in the past, it's time to learn to walk in the law of the God, day and night, to "do business" in your God-provided authority, and to operate in true freedom. The message of the gate hanging is very much like the message of Jesus in John 8:

> Then Jesus said to those Jews who believed Him, "If you abide in My word, you are My disciples indeed. And you shall know the truth, and the truth shall make you free.... Most assuredly, I say to you, whoever commits sin is a slave of sin. And a slave does not abide in the house forever, but a son abides forever. Therefore if the Son makes you free, you shall be free indeed."
>
> —John 8:31–36

Will the truth set you free? Absolutely! And when it does, God's truth will keep you free. A new ability to stand in His liberty is assured. You can maintain your position in Christ confidently and continually as you abide under His lordship and receive new power in a day-to-day "self-governing"—established, strong, and stable.

PLACING THE GATES

When some people read the Book of Nehemiah, they read verse 15 of chapter 6 to mean that the entire wall-building project was completed in a miraculously short fifty-two-day time period. Here's what it says: "So the wall was finished on the twenty-fifth day of Elul, in fifty-two days" (Neh. 6:15).

It was the gate-hanging process itself that took fifty-two days (possibly only forty-five days if you take out the Sabbaths)—a time period that is impressively efficient for hanging ten massive gates. The reason it's worded this way is because the wall was considered finished at last when the last of the gates was hung.

It would have been utterly impossible for the entire wall building plus gate hanging to occur in less than two months, especially considering the all-out devastation that confronted the rebuilders at the beginning. A century and a half earlier, Nebuchadnezzar's destruction of Jerusalem had been complete, and the restoration process had been neglected for a further ninety years after the Jews had returned.

Besides, we have been told in the previous chapter that Nehemiah served as governor of the city of Jerusalem for twelve years (Neh. 5:14). This, apparently, is the length of leave-time he had requested of King Artaxerxes. (See Nehemiah 2:6.)

We find no single statement that summarizes how much time had been devoted to rebuilding the stone walls, but there is an abundance of evidence that the task was wearying in the extreme, indicating that it took an extended period of time.

The beginning of Nehemiah 6 does testify to the swift completion of the gate raising. It opens with a comment that the ten gates were all that remained to be finished, and verse 15 gives the date of final completion, about seven weeks later.

GLORY IN THE GATES

At last the gates were in place!

The city had been refortified, and it was beautiful to behold. Now if the leaders and the citizens could only remain steadfast in their commitments and law-abiding in their decisions, they would be able to reap all of the benefits of the extended rebuilding process.

As is often the case with a major project, a time of celebration and formal dedication was set for the immediate future, and Nehemiah turned his attention to the affairs of government. He himself could not stay in Jerusalem; he needed to return to the capital city of the empire. First he needed to find his own replacement, so he turned over the governorship to his brother Hanani, the same one who had first brought the news about the state of Jerusalem to the palace in Shushan twelve years earlier:

> Then it was, when the wall was built and I had hung the doors, when the gatekeepers, the singers, and the Levites had been appointed, that I gave the charge of Jerusalem to my brother Hanani, and Hananiah the leader of the citadel, for he was a faithful man and feared God more than many. And I said to them, "Do not let the gates of Jerusalem be opened until the sun is hot; and while they stand guard, let them shut and bar the doors; and appoint guards from among the inhabitants of Jerusalem, one at his watch station and another in front of his own house."
>
> —NEHEMIAH 7:1–3

Nehemiah's instructions are based on the fact that the gates represent control from *within* the city. At this point, to breach the gates would mean invasion by a foreign power. Whoever controlled the gates would control the city.

Think about how much this is like our own lives. When the Holy Spirit is able to express His grace in every aspect of our lives (via every "gate"), the kingdom of God is gloriously manifest.

It's one thing to be a saved soul. It's another, much better, thing to be a growing, fully functional child of the living God, as secure in the pragmatics of your life as you are secure in the mightiness of His grace.

When the Holy Spirit is allowed to complete His rebuilding work in your life, you find that you can maintain the rebuilt walls and gates of your soul in all of their beauty and dignity, as long as you obey His instructions for your day-to-day conduct.

Although the Holy Spirit will never leave you as Nehemiah left Jerusalem to return to the palace, God does want you to assume a new role of responsibility in your life. Hanani, originally a picture of an intercessor when he came to Shushan to ask for Nehemiah's help, will be the one who will govern Jerusalem by walking in Nehemiah's instructions. This is not much different from the way you and I need to ask for help to "walk in the Spirit" every day.

We can read about the establishment of sound government for Jerusalem in chapters 10 and 11 of the Book of Nehemiah. This is parallel to the establishment of the full, Spirit-formed kingdom of God in our lives.

The kingdom of God is not just a place in heaven. It's not a reference to religious enterprise or activity. Rather, it is that phrase that references the will or rule of God, fully available and active in your life as you continue in His grace and power.

Here's what Nehemiah and Hanani led the people to do:

> Then the rest of the people—the priests, Levites, gatekeepers, singers, Temple servants, and all who had separated themselves from the pagan people of the land in order to obey the Law of God, together with their wives, sons, daughters, and all who were old enough to understand—joined their leaders and…solemnly promised to carefully follow all the commands, regulations, and decrees of the LORD our Lord.
>
> —NEHEMIAH 10:28–29, NLT

They were declaring their intention to walk according to God's law and to accept the consequences of walking otherwise. This was not a superstitious exercise or one that was forced upon them. Men, women, and children, all were free to declare that they wanted God's rule in their lives together. They were learning the truth of God's ways and the joy of following Him.

Let's extend the application to ourselves as well. Make your declaration the same as theirs as you affirm and maintain your wholehearted desire to become fully like your Master.

Chapter 16

FACING TOMORROW WITH JOY

BREATHE DEEPLY. DO IT again, please. Now, touch the most solid object near you and answer this question: Which of these two is the most important to sustaining your life—breath or material things?

Simple to answer, isn't it? Breath, of course. Without breathing we cannot live. Our bodies need a constant supply of oxygen, and it's important for our lungs and respiratory system to work efficiently.

It's the same with the breath of God's Spirit, infused with His Word, which together are the source and sustaining power of our spiritual lives.

The one thing in this world that you and I can touch with our fingers that has "eternity" written into its fabric is the Word of God. Every time I take a Bible in hand, I hold eternity, because the life force inherent in the Word exceeds all time and space. Jesus said, "Heaven and earth will pass away, but My Word shall not pass away." (See Mark 13:31.)

Those words hold the seeds of life. Your life becomes durable, fulfilling, and successful in direct proportion to the degree that the Word of God becomes as vital to you.

The Gospel of John says of Jesus that "the Word became flesh…" (John 1:14). The Word of God is the source of all substance and life. "In the beginning God created…" (Gen. 1:1). He did that with His Word. Christ was there at Creation: "In the beginning was the Word" (John 1:1).

All that is, as well as all that ever shall be, flows to man by Jesus Christ through the Word of God!

Responding to God's Word

Chapter 8 of the Book of Nehemiah records the response of a people who rediscovered the Word of God, misunderstood it, responded exactly backward to it, and then received help from Nehemiah toward a God-intended response. Once again, the record of their experience can help us in our lives today.

I want to do my utmost to ensure that you know how to keep on receiving the Word of God. I don't mean how to read it, how to memorize it, or how to study it, though all of those practices are very important. My primary concern is that your input and application of the Word—as the life-giving breath of God, the very Spirit of the Word—will fill and fulfill your soul continually. It's the only way to keep the "rebuilt you" built up and expanding.

The Word of God is not simply information or facts. It is a living Word, and it is life giving, healing, protecting, and invincible. You need to know how to let it work in you. If the Word's reality is at work in you, there is no way you will ever be less than filled with abundant life and fruitful living. (See 2 Peter 1:4, 8.)

EZRA READS THE LAW

Preliminary to the dedication of the completed walls, Nehemiah enlisted the help of the priest Ezra to present the Word of God to all the people. A two-day event was scheduled and logistical arrangements made, including preparation of a high platform from which the readers and teachers could more easily be seen by everyone.

Ezra's name, by the way, means "aid." It's almost as if his name is "Helper." His job is to lead the people to the Word of God and to help them understand it. This is very much what the Holy Spirit does for us today. We have His help, as the Jews had Ezra's help. We also have His bracing comfort, as the Jews had the encouragement of Nehemiah (whose name, you will remember, means "comforter," which is another one of the names for the Holy Spirit).

In those days people did not have their own Bibles. "Bibles" would have been handwritten scrolls, and not only did most of them not own such scrolls, but they also could not read anyway. In fact, scrolls of the Law were rare, even among the priests, and these people had not heard the Word read for years. Some of them had *never* been exposed to it. It's hard for us to conceive of such a degree of separation from the Word of God.

The people were thrilled to be hearing this reading. They stood riveted to every word of the Law. They worshiped and gave thanks, lifting up their hands in praise, and then they remained standing together for several hours, just listening to the reading. The whole scene is one of gratitude and reverence for the Word of God. Adding to it all was the careful explanation given by those who "gave the sense" of what had been clearly read from the Law, helping the people understand its meaning.

Then, what began so joyously suddenly reversed. People began to weep mournfully. Apparently, as they heard the words of the Law, they were overwhelmed by recognition of their own violations and their inadequacy to fulfill the commandments. The situation was one most church leaders would revel in: a repentant, sensitive response to the awareness that God's commands had been neglected. Here was the obvious fruit of awakened understanding and impassioned concern.

Or was it? Amazingly, Nehemiah and Ezra *stopped* this demonstration of grief. They spoke correctively to the people, insisting that since "this is a holy day," mourning and weeping were inappropriate.

It's mind-boggling. Here is a total reversal of what you would expect to see. Then, as though stopping tears of repentance weren't enough, the two leaders begin to stir the people toward celebration: "Go your way, eat the fat, drink the sweet, and send portions to those for whom nothing is prepared; for this day is holy to our Lord" (Neh. 8:10).

It's party time? Yes, it was time to celebrate. The people shifted their mood and their response. As it turned out, they progressed to a full-scale, weeklong observance of the ancient Feast of Tabernacles.

What should we think of this? Evidently, even though the following chapter was dedicated entirely to the record of the people's confession of sin, with fasting and manifest repentance, the Holy Spirit wanted the people to receive His Word as blessed nourishment and joy-filled encouragement—not as a source of mourning.

It's *right* to confess our sins, but don't sink into condemnation or confusion. Confusion about the confession of sin brings condemnation to those who don't understand the liberating truth of the Word.

> But if we walk in the light as He is in the light, we have fellowship with one another, and the blood of Jesus Christ His Son cleanses us from all sin. If we say that we have no sin, we deceive ourselves, and the truth is not in us. If we confess our sins, He is faithful and just to forgive us our sins and to cleanse us from all unrighteousness.
>
> —1 JOHN 1:7–9

It's good to step into the light. The light and warmth of God's Word and the fellowship of Jesus's own presence will point us to those stains or sin that can soil or restrict our growth in His life and love. He wants them to be washed away, allowing His grace through the cross to release us to an ongoing advance toward all He has for us.

So, let's learn the balance. Do invite the Holy Spirit's purification, often praying as David did in Psalm 139:23–24:

> Search me, O God, and know my heart; try me, and know my anxieties; and see if there is any wicked way in me, and lead me in the way everlasting.
>
> —PSALM 139:23–24

In praying that way, make no mistake when you see the word *wicked*. It jumps out at us, and some may miss the promise and the hope it is pointing toward. If sin is present, remember, "We have an Advocate with the Father, Jesus Christ the righteous" (1 John 2:1).

And it's unto Jesus, who stands before the Father in our behalf, that the Holy Spirit wants to bring us whenever He corrects or convicts us of anything twisted, deceived, or distorted (i.e., *wicked*). His objective? Never to condemn but always to lead the cleansing, deliverance, and liberty.

> There is therefore now no condemnation to those who are in Christ Jesus, who do not walk according to the flesh, but according to the Spirit. For the law of the Spirit of life in Christ Jesus has made me free from the law of sin and death. For what the law could not do in that it was weak through the flesh, God did by sending His own Son in the likeness of sinful flesh, on account of sin: He condemned sin in the flesh, that the righteous requirement of the law might be fulfilled in us who do not walk according to the flesh but according to the Spirit.
>
> —Romans 8:1–4

Let us relive the Book of Nehemiah! Right after the weeping stops and the rejoicing begins, we find one of the most encouraging sentences in all of the Bible: "The joy of the Lord is your strength" (Neh. 8:10).

We can *begin* by rejoicing, knowing the "promise power" in His commandments. The same Word that rebukes us will also release us! The Law that guides us will also fuel our souls with a dynamic for living.

"He who calls you is faithful, who also will do it" (1 Thess. 5:24)—a promise that when God gives an assignment to us, His words include enablement.

"No word of God shall be without power" (Luke 1:37, AMP). This verse, translated elsewhere, "For with God nothing will be impossible," is a mighty statement. It tells us that every word God speaks contains the power needed to actuate it. Every word of His that directs our behavior also makes the new behavior possible.

This is why Paul assures the Philippians, "It is God who works in you both to will and to do for His good pleasure" (Phil. 2:13).

This is truly a reason for joy. It builds our repentance upon the foundation of deep, trusting faith rather than upon guilt and emotionalism.

The godly repentance shown in Nehemiah 9, following the feasting and rejoicing encouraged by their leaders, verifies that a joyous response to God's Word is not adverse to a repentant spirit but complementary to it.

In His parable of the sower, Jesus speaks of those who hear the Word and receive it with joy, but because they don't let it take root in themselves, it doesn't bear fruit. (See Matthew 13:18–23.) The fact that He describes these as cases where shallowness of soul brought no abiding fruit doesn't imply that receiving the Word with joy was at fault, but that lack of depth and abiding was the problem. In other words, depth and joyousness can go together.

THE COMFORT OF THE COMFORTER

A few years into my pastorate at The Church On The Way, a new understanding began to dawn on my soul. I was seeking the Lord for guidance concerning my own teaching ministry and inquiring of Him specifically concerning the mood and manner of our congregation's worship services.

For much of my life, reverence at worship was basically defined as "silence," and the expected sign of God's presence with power was "uncomfortable sinners"—people squirming under conviction.

I had seen times when His awesome presence had genuinely inspired us to, "Be still, and know that [He is] God" (Ps. 46:10), and I had also seen sinners cringe as the sword of the Spirit pierced their souls. I had always believed that God intended these reactions to be normative.

However, as silence usually prevailed, worship was usually perfunctory. And although souls were born again, there were few saved by reason of having been gripped by inner conviction. Was this "normal" worship in God's eyes? I began to ask, "Lord, what should be the atmosphere among a people who worship You and where Your Word is faithfully preached?"

God began to answer me from His Word: "Comfort, yes, comfort My people!…Speak comfort to Jerusalem, and cry out to her, that her warfare is ended" (Isa. 40:1–2).

The more I thought on this and studied the context of Isaiah's prophecy, the more I began to see the sunlight of a truth I had never quite perceived before: God wants people to be *happy* in His presence! Our "warfare has ended" because our Redeemer has come! The continued call throughout the psalms is to praise and rejoice before the Lord: "In Your presence is fullness of joy; at Your right hand are pleasures forevermore" (Ps. 16:11). In the same spirit, Paul insists of the Philippians, "Rejoice in the Lord alway: and again I say, Rejoice" (Phil. 4:4, kjv).

The result of my quest was a slow but definite transformation in my approach to leading our services. It wasn't as though I had been negative or dismal, but I began to invite and model a new brightness. It was not superficial promotion but a joyful atmosphere birthed by the confidence that when we are happy in His presence, it makes God happy too!

I soon found people responded with greater faith and commitment, and they steadily moved forward in definitive growth. Not only did our services become healthy times of celebration in worship and in the Word, but also hearts and homes began to flourish in the warmth of God's love and joy. Somehow, without our realizing it at the time, Ezra and Nehemiah's instruction was being lived out among people who were beginning to learn the wisdom of receiving the Word of God with joy.

Today, when repentance is needed (and so often it is), we repent; when a new call to holiness is issued, we obey; when the depths of our hearts are plumbed, sensitive response is shown. But the predominant atmosphere in our worship services is one of sound-minded, balanced joyfulness, and the biblical fruit of that joy is seen everywhere: "For the joy of the LORD is [our] strength" (Neh. 8:10).

REJOICE!

Joy is the heartbeat of the good news concerning the birth of our Lord: "Behold, I bring you good tidings of great joy, which shall be to all people. For unto you is born this day...a Saviour, which is Christ the Lord" (Luke 2:10–11, KJV).

- The news is good—"I bring you good tidings."
- The joy is great—"of great joy...to all people."
- The focus is you—"for unto you."

- The time is now—"is born this day…a Saviour."
- And God is here—"which is Christ the Lord."

Dear friend, I want to send you into all your tomorrows with the Word of God in your hand and the joy of the Lord in your heart. Yes, His Word is absolute authority and, yes, He absolutely calls us to obedience in following Jesus Christ. And joy is appropriate when that same Word is received and becomes strength to your soul. When you have said, "Yes, Lord," to His Word, there is every reason to begin rejoicing at once. You need not wait until perfection is secured, for His welcomed Word will work progressively and mightily in you to accomplish the Father's pleasure. And you can rejoice now over that!

The Word that created all worlds is the Word that is completing you. Rest in that assurance, and rejoice in His Word as He "rebuilds the real you," the "you" He intended when He created you.

Centuries ago, a band of battered people stood facing the embarrassing evidence of their inability to recover the ruins of their past.

Then a helper came.

Don't miss seeing this helper. He's there in the story of Nehemiah, and He's here today in your life: the Holy Spirit. The Holy Spirit is ready now to take you from this moment onward toward the fulfillment of Father God's high destiny for you. Rebirth, redemption, restoration, and recovery are only a part of His mission. He wants to bring you to the full realization of God's purposes, patterns, and promises for your life.

Chapter 17

THE PRACTICE OF WORSHIP

T HE DAY OF THE dedication of the rebuilt wall was a joyous one:

Now at the dedication of the wall of Jerusalem they sought out the Levites in all their places, to bring them to Jerusalem to celebrate the dedication with gladness, both with thanksgivings and singing, with cymbals and stringed instruments and harps. And the sons of the singers gathered together from the countryside around Jerusalem, from the villages of the Netophathites, from the house of Gilgal, and from the fields of Geba and Azmaveth; for the singers had built themselves villages all around Jerusalem. Then the priests and Levites purified themselves, and purified the people, the gates, and the wall.

So I brought the leaders of Judah up on the wall, and appointed two large thanksgiving choirs.

—NEHEMIAH 12:27–31

The text goes on to name the singers, priests, and trumpeters who comprised the two thanksgiving choirs. From their starting place, they processed around the walls in opposite directions toward the temple, making such a loud and joyful sound that they could be heard for miles around (v. 43). One of the choirs was accompanied by the musical instruments that had been saved from King David's collection (v. 36). The two groups of worshipers converged at the temple, where the priests offered great sacrifices in celebration and dedication of the great work that had been accomplished.

This was more than a one-time event, and it was far more than the one-line "dedication" we have by the frontispiece of a book. This dedication was a turning point. It was as if the people were turning a fresh page on their corporate life, declaring for all the world to see that they intended to live lives befitting of their new status.

Their worship pointed to the mighty God who had helped them so greatly. He had enabled them to complete a task that had appeared to be impossible. From now on—and we can declare this with them as we move forward with our newly reconstructed personalities—they would walk a Spirit-formed, Spirit-filled walk, beginning every day and every week with heartfelt praise. Their praise would keep breaking the back of accusation and condemnation, as will ours. What a day!

Built Up to Grow Up

The Jews and their leaders had been "built up to grow up," as we said in chapter 14, just as their new wall had been built to last.

They had entered into a new covenant with their God. From here on out, everything would be perfect...or would it? Can that ever happen?

Of course, God will keep His part of the new covenant, but, of course, the people will not. It seems to be equally impossible for us to do so as well, despite the fact that we have achieved genuine progress and the walls of our souls have been truly rebuilt. The Jerusalem Jews were about to prove the truth that the writer of the Hebrews expressed much later: "The LORD disciplines those he loves, and he punishes each one he accepts as his child" (Heb. 12:6, NLT).

They would soon discover, when Nehemiah was forced to discipline them, the truth of Proverbs 3:11–12:

> Do not despise the chastening of the LORD,
> Nor detest His correction;
> For whom the LORD loves He corrects,
> Just as a father the son in whom he delights.

Yes, just as Nehemiah is a picture of the Holy Spirit in action, rebuilding your personality and protecting you from harm, so He also becomes a picture of the Holy Spirit as the expression of the Father's discipline.

Nehemiah came to scrutinize the Jews of Jerusalem just as the Holy Spirit comes to monitor your ongoing walk with God. When He sees compromises and unfaithfulness rise up within you and get in the way of what was intended to be the glorious and blessed purpose of God in your life, He will be patient for a while, and then He will finally say, in essence, "Look, I'm not going to put up with this," and He will become firm with you.

He does it because He is grieved and He wants you to come back to Him, not because He wants to disassociate with you or banish you. Remember Ephesians 4:30: "Do not grieve the Holy Spirit of God, by whom you were sealed for the day of redemption." But if you do grieve Him, He will let you know about it, and He will tell you what to do about it too.

In fact, if He does not come to you with a rod of correction from time to time, this will be evidence that you are not a legitimate child: "If you are without chastening, of which all have become partakers, then you are illegitimate and not sons" (Heb. 12:8).

Therefore, you can expect some correction. It is to be hoped, however, that your discipline will not replicate the punishment that Nehemiah dished out!

NEHEMIAH RIDES AGAIN

In chapter 13 we find a second case of Nehemiah's anger as he was forced to deal with irresponsibility and disobedience among the people. The first case was just before the gates were hung and the wall dedicated, but the second is sometime after he had completed the project, resumed his post in Persia, and then returned for a brief visit to Jerusalem.

Nehemiah's visit is shocking to the point of being humorous— that is, as long as you weren't one of the recipients of his correction! One day I happened to read this part of the story in the Living Bible. How would you have liked to be on the receiving end of this?

> I [Nehemiah] realized that some of the Jews had married women from Ashdod, Ammon, and Moab, and that many

of their children spoke in the language of Ashdod and couldn't speak the language of Judah at all. So I confronted these parents and cursed them and punched a few of them and knocked them around and pulled out their hair; and they vowed before God that they would not let their children intermarry with non-Jews.

"Wasn't this exactly King Solomon's problem?" I demanded. "There was no king who could compare with him, and God loved him and made him the king over all Israel; but even so he was led into idolatry by foreign women. Do you think that we will let you get away with this sinful deed?"

—NEHEMIAH 13:23–27, TLB

That isn't all.

Nehemiah also discovered that refuge had been given to the evil Tobiah—and in the temple itself, of all places! Other compromises had also been made in his absence, and Nehemiah moved with boldness and decisive action:

Eliashib the priest, who had been appointed as custodian of the Temple storerooms and who was also a good friend of Tobiah, had converted a storage room into a beautiful guest room for Tobiah. The room had previously been used for storing the grain offerings, frankincense, bowls, and tithes of grain, new wine, and olive oil....

I was not in Jerusalem at the time, for I had returned to Babylon in the thirty-second year of the reign of King Artaxerxes (though I later received his permission to go back again to Jerusalem). When I arrived back in Jerusalem and learned of this evil deed of Eliashib—that he had prepared a guest room in the Temple for Tobiah—I was very upset and threw out all of his belongings from the room. Then I demanded that the room be thoroughly cleaned, and I brought back the Temple bowls, the grain offerings, and frankincense.

I also learned that the Levites had not been given what was due them, so they and the choir singers who were supposed to conduct the worship services had returned to their farms. I immediately confronted the leaders and demanded, "Why has the Temple been forsaken?" Then I called all the Levites back again and restored them to their proper duties. And once more all the people of Judah began bringing their tithes of grain, new wine, and olive oil to the Temple treasury....

One day I was on a farm and saw some men treading winepresses on the Sabbath, hauling in sheaves, and loading their donkeys with wine, grapes, figs, and all sorts of produce which they took that day into Jerusalem. So I opposed them publicly. There were also some men from Tyre bringing fish and all sorts of wares and selling them on the Sabbath to the people of Jerusalem.

Then I asked the leaders of Judah, "Why are you profaning the Sabbath? Wasn't it enough that your fathers did this sort of thing and brought the present evil days upon us and upon our city? And now you are bringing more wrath upon the people of Israel by permitting the Sabbath to be desecrated in this way."

So from then on I commanded that the gates of the city be shut as darkness fell on Friday evenings and not be opened until the Sabbath had ended; and I sent some of my servants to guard the gates so that no merchandise could be brought in on the Sabbath day. The merchants and tradesmen camped outside Jerusalem once or twice, but I spoke sharply to them and said, "What are you doing out here, camping around the wall? If you do this again, I will arrest you." And that was the last time they came on the Sabbath....

One of the sons of Jehoiada (the son of Eliashib the High Priest) was a son-in-law of Sanballat the Horonite, so I chased him out of the Temple. Remember them, O my God, for they have defiled the priesthood and the promises and vows of the priests and Levites. So I purged out the foreigners and assigned tasks to the priests and Levites, making certain that each knew his work.

—Nᴇʜᴇᴍɪᴀʜ 13:4–12, 15–21, 28–30, ᴛʟʙ

"Stuff" certainly had a way of creeping in, didn't it? We don't know how long Nehemiah was away from Jerusalem, but it didn't seem to take long for the people to revert to their former ways—and then some.

This matter of Tobiah, for instance, was far more than a disagreement about social courtesy. Tobiah was a traitor to his own people. He was Jewish, but he was part of the "triumvirate" with Sanballat and Geshem, and he had done everything in his power to oppose the rebuilding of the wall. How did this thing happen? Nobody ever seems to know how these things happen. How does it happen when we "give room" to thoughts and habits that we had once repudiated as ungodly?

Here a relative of the high priest had opened up a special storeroom for the use of a traitor, removing the implements of worship and sacrifice to the Lord. It was unthinkable; the guy who had been absolutely resistant to every step of the reestablishment of the city of God had been given free rent in the worship center!

But don't we have this same capacity? Each of us fits the description in Ephesians 4 (right before the line about not grieving the Holy Spirit) that adjures us not to "give place to the devil" (Eph. 4:27).

When Nehemiah makes his discoveries, he doesn't procrastinate at all. He doesn't say, "Let's negotiate." He barges in and starts throwing things out. There's something about this that reminds us of the impatience of God with concessions to the adversary's purpose in our life. There are things that we should be able to identify as evil, and it is our business to resist them.

We may say, "Oh, I just love to come to worship. The Spirit's presence is so sweet. I love what I feel." And then the Holy Spirit starts to stir things up and throw things out. We are baffled. "I don't know what's happening. I was so happy last night at church, and today all these things are backfiring on me. Oh, pray for me; the devil is against me."

No, the devil isn't at fault. The Holy Spirit has come against you this time. He's saying, "You have given place to darkness, and I will not let you partner with it." Be frank with yourself. Look at your heart and admit where you have replaced the implements of true worship with sorry substitutes. Let the Holy Spirit's chastening have its full effect so you can get back to where you were before.

Worship Washout

Then Nehemiah discovered that the people had stopped bringing the offerings for worship that would have allowed worship to continue

(Neh. 13:10–13). He asked, "Why is the place of God forsaken?" and he addressed their failure to tithe, their failure to make sure that worship was sustained in the temple, and their failure to supply the "worship teams" with the support that God had mandated.

This touches on the matter of our giving and coming regularly to the house of the Lord to worship with other believers. To neglect to gather with the people of the Lord is confronted in Scripture: "Do not forsake the assembling of yourselves together, as is the manner of some, but exhort one another" (Heb. 10:25, author's paraphrase).

The Bible summons us to be people of worship. It's something the Holy Spirit will goad you about, and it's important to receive that instruction and to live in its wisdom. Scripture directs us to tithe as well, and the Spirit won't excuse a casual attitude. ("Well, you know, I'm just kind of serving the Lord as well as I know how.")

To that, the Holy Spirit says, "Well, if that's all you know how to do, I'll teach you better." He won't tolerate what is alien or hostile in the place of worship, and He won't let you fail to contribute what is necessary to your worship life.

THE SABBATH SELLOUT

In the Old Testament, the observance of the Sabbath was a direct expression of the people's covenant with God. So when we see, as we do in Nehemiah 13:15–22, a violent reaction to Sabbath-breaking, it will help us to understand how significant that was.

Nehemiah got up on his first Sabbath back in Jerusalem, and what did he see? The gates were opened wide and sellers of all kinds of goods came on in for another day's commerce. The people of the city opened their shops. Nehemiah blew his stack.

The people paid attention when he started shouting. This was the same Nehemiah who had put the city back together. He had come back for a visit, and they recognized him—as he confronted them at every turn.

Then, even though the city officials had conceded that Nehemiah was right and they made the people close their shops, ushered the sellers out, and closed the city gates, the businesspeople, especially the ones from up the coast in Tyre, just didn't budge. They lingered outside the gates, and the next week they returned on the Sabbath as if nothing had changed. Not doing business on the Sabbath was cutting into their profits big-time. They were not interested in following somebody's new rules.

Nehemiah stood up on the wall and yelled down to them, in essence, "You guys clear out of here or I'm going to come down there personally and punch out your lights." He was angry. This is the one we called "the comforter"?

COVENANT BREAKERS

Understand, please, that Nehemiah's anger was not merely over the people's disobedience and foolishness, as bad as that was. His fury arose primarily over the fact that these same people had made specific commitments not to do the things they were now doing.

In other words, these were not the acts of ignorance. They knew better. Moreover, they had publicly confessed, with much regret, the fact that they had walked in such disobedience in the past. Nehemiah chapter 9 elaborates their repentance in the light of God's great mercy and grace, and chapter 10 lists the names of those who led in sealing a covenant of obedience to walk according to God's law.

But now Nehemiah had discovered their retreat from that covenant, and he refused to allow them to violate their commitment to God. His anger was not against them, but he used it to shock and shake them back to that place where their best interests could be served through fidelity toward the Lord.

Years of pastoring have taught me that the healing and deliverance of human souls can only be preserved where responsible obedience is manifest by those receiving the Holy Spirit's rebuilding within them. Nehemiah's anger and actions are fully appropriate, and they reveal God's heart concerning known violations of His foundational principles.

Jesus's words to the restored include this advice, which we are wise to heed:

Now you are well; so stop sinning, or something even worse may happen to you.

—JOHN 5:14, NLT

When an unclean spirit goes out of a man, he goes through dry places, seeking rest; and finding none, he says, "I will return to my house from which I came." And when he comes, he finds it swept and put in order. Then he goes and takes with him seven other spirits more wicked than himself, and they enter and dwell there; and the last state of that man is worse than the first.

—LUKE 11:24–26

These are hard words. But Jesus also said, "Neither do I condemn you; go and sin no more" (John 8:11).

Rebuilt and Living a Restored Life

What should we do with all of this?

Well, for one thing, thank the Holy Spirit that He is jealous enough to crowd you against the wall. Give thanks to God that He cares enough about you to not allow you to wander off the narrow but joy-filled pathway of holiness and true abundant living.

When you feel overwhelmed by the circumstances of life, ask Him to show you what He's doing. He wants to get your attention. He will not allow you to be defeated by your Sanballat, your Tobiah, your Geshem, or your own wayward human impulses.

Then, once you hear His voice saying, "Come," return to Him. Come back. He will bring the power of the cleansing blood of Jesus that not only carries away the stains of sin but also filters out whatever is toxic to His new life. He will identify the hidden works of darkness. He will dissolve bondages. He will not permit you to continue to grieve the Spirit. He is your permanent Helper.

He who has come to help you see your life rebuilt will also come to see your life advanced into His purposes. He will respond to your every prayer, and He will nurture your soul, reminding you of His loving character and His clear truth.

The Holy Spirit, your Nehemiah, will restore, establish, strengthen, and settle you, today and every day of the rest of your life.

Give Him thanks and worship!

Appendix A

MAP OF JERUSALEM AND SPIRIT/ SOUL/BODY DIAGRAM

THE FOLLOWING DIAGRAMS ILLUSTRATE the parallel between the destroyed walls and the wounded personality (the soul).

- The restored *temple* is parallel to the restored and reborn human *spirit*.
- The *walls* of the city are parallel to the fortification of the human *soul*.
- The surrounding land of Israel is parallel to the human *body*.

Now may the God of peace Himself sanctify you completely; and may your whole spirit, soul, and body be preserved blameless at the coming of our Lord Jesus Christ.

—1 THESSALONIANS 5:23

This pairing of diagrams conveys the idea of the ravaged walls and the shattered soul.

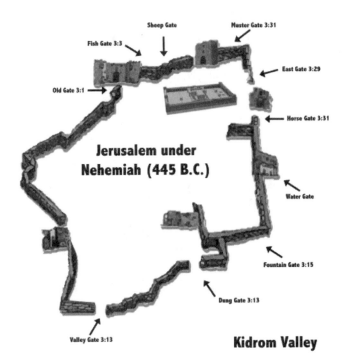

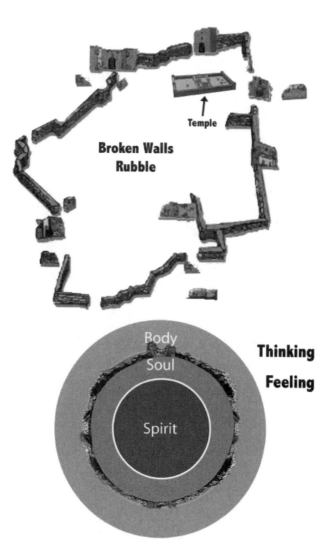

Appendix B

HISTORICAL NOTES

B ECAUSE THE AVERAGE BIBLE reader has difficulty envisioning the historic placement of the Book of Nehemiah, it is generally bypassed in study. Besides this fact, it contains several censuses (Neh. 7:4–73; 11:1–36; 12:1–26), genealogies (Neh. 12:1–26), uninviting passages with difficult names listed (Neh. 3:1–32; 12:32–47), and the apparent repetition of history recorded elsewhere (Neh. 9:5–38). The adjacent time line and the following brief remarks are intended to help orient you to the place of Nehemiah in Bible history.

Babylon held world dominance for a very short time (c. 605–539 B.C.), but Nebuchadnezzar, the king who gained that dominance, was the instrument God used to judge Judah (Southern Kingdom) and bring about the destruction of Jerusalem. The fall of Babylon took place under Nebuchadnezzar's grandson, Belshazzar, by an overthrow—an engineering/military tactic of phenomenal proportion—executed in one night according to Daniel's prophecy (Dan. 5). The overthrow was accomplished by Cyrus, the Medo-Persian leader.

Cyrus (see Isaiah, noted below) released the first contingent of exiles desiring to return to Jerusalem/Judah. He ruled the Persian

Empire until Darius (rule: 521–486 B.C.), who was followed by Xerxes (rule: 486–465 B.C.) and Artaxerxes (rule: 465–424 B.C.), in whose court we find Nehemiah.

Historical Time Line (B.C.)	
Abraham	c. 2000
Isaac	c. 1950
Jacob (to Egypt)	c. 1830
Moses	c. 1520
The Exodus	c. 1440
Entry to Canaan	c. 1400
David	c. 1020
Divided Kingdom	c. 940
Northern Kingdom falls	727
Southern Kingdom falls	606–586
Babylon falls	539
First exiles return and begin rebuilding the temple	536
Complete temple	516
Second exiles return	457
Nehemiah to Jerusalem	444

Interaction of Some Prophets in the Course of History Surrounding the Exile and the Return From Captivity

Isaiah (c. 740–680 B.C.). Incredibly, the prophet Isaiah correctly named the monarch whom God would use to liberate the Jews (Isa. 45:1).

Jeremiah (events: 626–587 B.C.). Among Jeremiah's prophecies is the specific statement numbering the years of Israel's captivity (Jer. 25:11).

Daniel (c. 618–535 B.C.). Daniel lived through the entire captivity. Reading Jeremiah one day, he began interceding for release (Dan. 9–10).

Haggai/Zechariah (events: 536–516 B.C.). Haggai also lived through the exile and returned. He and Zechariah stirred the people to rebuild the temple.

Ezra (events: c. 536–450 B.C.). As a historian, Ezra recorded the first return of exiles under Zerubbabel (536 B.C.). As a priest, he led the second contingent (457 B.C.) and was later joined by Nehemiah.

Nehemiah (events: c. 444–430 B.C.). Nehemiah was a consultant to Artaxerxes, emperor of the Persian Empire, when, as a godly Jewish patriot, he asked for permission to assist the condition of the returned exiles. He helped them for twelve years.

HOW LONG WAS THE PROJECT?

The chronology of this Book of Nehemiah is complicated, and some difference of opinion exists by reason of apparent conflicts in the text. The seeming inconsistencies resolve when simple reasoning is added to one literary practice common to Hebrew literature: the *prolepsis.* A prolepsis is something written in anticipation of what follows: "The introduction into a narrative of events as taking place before it could have done so, or the treating of a future event as if it had already happened" (Webster). An example of this is in Nehemiah 3:1, where the walls are described as completed and the doors as having been hung, whereas Nehemiah clearly writes in chapter 6, verse 1 of the doors as not yet being set in place.

A combination of references is helpful in solving the question, "How long was the building project in progress?"

Some have made the sincere mistake of concluding from Nehemiah 6:15 that the total rebuilding of the walls of Jerusalem took place in fifty-two days. This is an utter impossibility in view of the complete devastation in Nehemiah 2:12–15. It is ludicrous to suppose that a task that could be completed in seven to eight weeks would have been neglected for ninety years.

What Nehemiah 6:15 does testify to is the duration of the time between Nehemiah 6:1 and the completion of the hanging of the doors in all the gates. Chapter 6 opens with mention that the gates were all that remained to be finished, and verse 15 indicates that this process was completed in a little over seven weeks—both a remarkable and reasonable time considering there were ten great gateways into the city.

We are specifically told by Nehemiah that he served the governorship of the city for a twelve-year period (Neh. 5:14), apparently the period of time he requested of Artaxerxes (Neh. 2:6). Exactly how much of this time was occupied in the recovery of the walls, until the final placement of the gates, we are never told in a summary statement. But we do know that aside from the delays caused by the resistance of Sanballat and company, the progress was slow enough to cause weariness and discouragement with the massive mounds of rubble (Neh. 4:10). Make no mistake: Nebuchadnezzar's troops had done their job well one hundred forty years before. Jerusalem was ransacked and left as a shame to its people. It was never intended for recovery, and the rebuilding was a massive task.

It is no discrediting of either God's grace among the Jews or Nehemiah's leadership of the project to suggest that it must have taken, at the very least, a number of years. Remember, the temple that they had already rebuilt had taken them twenty years to build.

Therefore, the idea of the rebuilding of the walls as a fifty-two-day "miracle" (actually forty-five days, removing Sabbaths as work days) is not mandated by the text. The grander miracle is displayed in the fact that notwithstanding so much opposition and such complete destruction, the tenacity of the leadership and the people persisted until the shame of nearly a century of neglect was overcome.

Appendix C

MAKING SURE THAT YOU
HAVE BEEN REBORN

THERE MAY BE SOME of you who, as you've been reading this book, have become aware of something unsettled in your own soul, a longing for an established confidence about your personal relationship with God. Have you been reborn? It's the first and most important step before any kind of reconstruction can take place in your life.

It is possible that until now you have never actually come to a specific moment in your life when you asked Jesus Christ to be your Savior. Have you ever personally invited Him into your heart?

Jesus said that unless we come to God in humility as children, we cannot truly begin in the life of God's kingdom:

> Assuredly, I say to you, unless you are converted and become as little children, you will by no means enter the kingdom of heaven. Therefore whoever humbles himself as this little child is the greatest in the kingdom of heaven.
>
> —MATTHEW 18:3–4

Have you knelt humbly and confessed your sin to God with child-like honesty? Have you prayed with childlike simplicity, inviting

Him to come into your heart? If you haven't before, then just pray now—simply and quietly—speaking these words with sincerity:

Holy Father God,

Depending on Jesus, I come to ask Your forgiveness for all my sin. I want Your will in my life and Your Word as my guide. Thank You for giving Your Son for my salvation. I now believe in and receive Him as my Savior and as my Lord. I receive Your love given to me through His death on the cross, and I receive Your life given to me by His resurrection from the dead. Lord Jesus Christ, come into my heart. Fill me with Your Holy Spirit, and let all my tomorrows increase in Your way from now unto eternity.

Amen.

Now pause a minute and praise God. Jesus Christ has just taken the reins of your life! Praise Him because:

1. All your sins are forgiven completely! (God says, "Their sins and iniquity I will remember against them no more." [See Hebrews 10:17].)

2. Complete peace with God has been established! ("Being justified by faith, we have peace with God through our Lord Jesus Christ" [Rom. 5:1, KJV].)

3. The courts of heaven resound with joy because of your salvation! (Jesus said there is joy in heaven over each sinner who repents. [See Luke 15:7].)

4. Your name is now written in the Book of Life! (The Book of Life is an actual registry in which God has listed all of us as His redeemed. [See Luke 10:20.])

5. You have an absolute hope of eternity in heaven! ("The gift of God is eternal life through Jesus Christ our Lord" [Rom. 6:23, KJV].)

6. Christ promises His daily presence and provision! ("I will never leave or forsake you.... I have come to give life abundantly." [See Hebrews 13:5; John 10:10.])

7. God has committed Himself to help you resist evil! ("And if God is for us, who can be against us?...We are more than conquerors through Him" [Rom. 8:31, 37].)

New life in Jesus Christ is yours forever, and these seven facts are only a few of the multiple guarantees you have from God—promises that secure confidence for your future. From here on out, God's Word gives firm footing for all your tomorrows. Whatever yet needs recovery, you have a solid and sufficient foundation in Christ. Rejoice and proceed with the rebuilding!

Pausing to insure your foundation in Christ is important because without your rebirth, the rebuilding project is an impossible task. Without secure footing through faith in the death and resurrection of the Lord Jesus, any attempts at building or rebuilding a life are destined for frustration and failure. "No other foundation can anyone lay than that which is laid, which is Jesus Christ" (1 Cor. 3:11).

In a real sense, rebirth and rebuilding are both new beginnings and foundational to true life in Christ.

The initial beginning point is the regeneration: "You must be born again" (John 3:7). This is virtually instantaneous, because everything about it has already been accomplished for us through Christ's death and resurrection: we are saved completely by His grace and His work (Eph. 2:8–9) and secured in the power of His perfected salvation for us (Titus 3:5).

The second beginning point is sanctification: "He who has begun a good work in you will keep performing it until the day Christ returns for you." (See Philippians 1:6.) This is a progressive program of growth and involves your responsible partnership with the Holy Spirit. It includes the Lord's promise to restore to us all that we have seen lost or destroyed in our past. (See Joel 2:23–29.) This has been the primary subject of this book.

Once the initial beginning is established—rebirth—you are ready for the second—rebuilding. Look at the examples in Israel's history. On two ancient occasions, the Jews found themselves troubled by circumstances in lands distant from their Promised Land of God's intended purpose.

The first was their sojourn in Egypt. After Jacob's family relocated during his son Joseph's influence there, later rulers reversed what had been a benevolent relationship. The Israelites' situation progressively deteriorated until later generations were put under slavery. Centuries later, under Moses, came their exodus, when the Lord delivered them, saying: "I...brought you out of Egypt, out of the house of bondage" (Exod. 20:2). Through the miracle of the Passover and the mighty display of their passage through the Red

Sea, they were liberated—a nation reborn and resurrected from death.

The second was their exile in Babylon. Following Jerusalem's destruction, the Jews were made political captives—a displaced people "marking time," as it were. But when the prophesied quota of years of judgment was fulfilled, the Lord brought them back to their ancestral home, returning them to the land of their inheritance and the city of their former rule.

Now, there is a vast and obvious difference in these two experiences. It's an instructive difference, much like the distinction between regeneration and sanctification—between being reborn and being rebuilt. For example:

1. In Egypt, they were slaves under brutal taskmasters. In Babylon, they were refugees, but with the opportunity of carrying on a somewhat normal enterprise.

2. In Egypt, their slavery was the result of their heredity. After successive generations, each one was simply born into bondage. In Babylon, their exile was the direct result of sinning, which produced their situation. They were a destroyed and displaced people.

Furthermore, the pathway to release in each case was different:

1. Deliverance from Egypt came through the blood of the Passover lamb.

2. Return from Babylon came by means of the king's edict, according to the prophecies of God's Word.

The relevance of contrasting Israel's Egyptian bondage and Babylonian captivity is that the rebuilding process we have been studying parallels the outcome of the latter event—their return from exile. That must be clearly seen because we should never suppose a person's new birth is a process—it isn't.

Our rebirth in Christ is a crisis, a moment in time when, like Israel's deliverance from Egypt, the blood of "the Lamb of God who takes away the sin of the world" (John 1:29) is acknowledged. That is our only hope of freedom from the bondage of sin.

However, following this, we all come to a time when we begin to deal with the fruit of past disobedience in the same way Israel's exiles returning from Babylon had to face the charred remains of Jerusalem, which was the direct result of past sinning.

First, the Lord Jesus Christ comes as Savior—the only solution to our deadness in sin, our lostness from and our guiltiness before God. His cross is the key to our redemption, and His resurrection power is the key to our receiving the gift of new life in Him.

Second, the Holy Spirit comes as Comforter—the One sent to help assist us in our helplessness, to instruct us beyond our ignorance, and to recover us from all our brokenness. His power is promised to us, and His leadership is given to assist us forward in our new life in Christ.

The Holy Spirit comes with all the equipment needed for our rebuilding, renewing, and recovering.

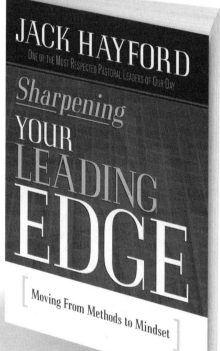